I0116763

As Long As There Are Slaughterhouses

There Will Be Wars

By
Dr. Sahadeva dasa

B.com., FCA., AICWA., PhD
Chartered Accountant

Soul Science University Press

www.kindnessClub.org

Readers interested in the subject matter of this
book are invited to correspond with the publisher at:
SoulScienceUniversity@gmail.com   +91 98490 95990
or visit DrDasa.com

First Edition: December 2014

Soul Science University Press expresses its gratitude to the
Bhaktivedanta Book Trust International (BBT), for the use of quotes by
His Divine Grace A.C.Bhaktivedanta Swami Prabhupada.

ISBN 97893-82947-19-6

Published by:
Dr. Sahadeva dasa for Soul Science University Press

Printed by:
Rainbow Print Pack, Hyderabad

To order a copy write to purnabramhadasa@gmail.com
or buy online: Amazon.com, rlbdeshop.com

By The Same Author

Oil-Final Countdown To A Global Crisis And Its Solutions
End of Modern Civilization And Alternative Future
To Kill Cow Means To End Human Civilization
Cow And Humanity - Made For Each Other
Cows Are Cool - Love 'Em!
Let's Be Friends - A Curious, Calm Cow
Wondrous Glories of Vraja
We Feel Just Like You Do
Tsunami Of Diseases Headed Our Way - Know Your Food Before Time
  Runs Out
Cow Killing And Beef Export - The Master Plan To Turn India Into A
  Desert
Capitalism Communism And Cowism - A New Economics For The 21st `
  Century
Noble Cow - Munching Grass, Looking Curious And Just Hanging Around
World - Through The Eyes Of Scriptures
To Save Time Is To Lengthen Life
Life Is Nothing But Time - Time Is Life, Life Is Time
Lost Time Is Never Found Again
Spare Us Some Carcasses - An Appeal From The Vultures
An Inch of Time Can Not Be Bought With A Mile of Gold
Cow Dung For Food Security And Survival of Human Race
Cow Dung – A Down To Earth Solution To Global Warming And
  Climate Change
Career Women - The Violence of Modern Jobs And The Lost Art of Home
  Making
Working Moms And Rise of A Lost Generation
Glories of Thy Wondrous Name
India A World Leader in Cow Killing And Beef Export - An Italian Did
  It In 10 Years
If Violence Must Stop, Slaughterhouses Must Close Down
Peak Soil – Industrial Civilization, On The Verge of Eating Itself
Corporatocracy : The New Gods – Greedy, Ruthless And Reckless
(More information on availability on DrDasa.com)

Contents

Preface

S avagery, much attributed to the 'old world' is not entirely absent in the 'new world' but rather it is more prevalent than ever before. Western civilization has made the 20th century the bloodiest century in human history. This civilization witnessed, besides the two most brutal World Wars, the worst acts of barbarism - holocaust, Gulag concentration camps, genocides and atomic bombing of Hiroshima and Nagasaki. Industrialization of wars and violence in the 20th century led to killing of more than 350 million people, directly or indirectly. Science and technology led to discovery and mass usage of lethal weapons. Usage of petroleum expanded the war zone to include several continents. Localized battles of 'old world' turned into global World wars.

But world wars haven't stopped for a moment. World has not seen respite from war. Right at this moment there are several countries fighting wars with one another. There is internal war going on in almost half of the countries in the world. All these wars are being fuelled and sustained by billions of tonnes of weapons produced by the Military-industrial complex every year. An impressive array of chemical, biological and nuclear weapons are waiting to be dropped on our heads. What has been produced at great cost and is being stored with great care, is certainly meant for use and will be used one day.

But why are we so hell-bent on killing each other? Why is our species so violence-prone? To answer these questions we would do well to think about our exploitation and slaughter of animals and its effect on human civilization. Could it be that we oppress and kill each other so readily because our abuse and slaughter of animals has desensitized us to the suffering and death of others? An ancient Chinese verse so rightly puts it, "For hundreds of thousands of years the stew in the pot has brewed hatred and resentment that is difficult to stop. If you wish to know why there are disasters of armies and weapons in the world, listen to the piteous cries from the slaughterhouse at midnight." Agnes Ryan concurs, "Wars will never cease while men still kill other animals for food, for to turn any living creature into a roast, a steak, a chop, or any other type of 'meat' takes the same kind of violence, the same kind of bloodshed, and the same kind of mental processes required to change a living man into a dead soldier."

Peace will be possible only if we live and let others live.

Sahedeva dasa

Dr. Sahadeva dasa
1st December 2014
Secunderabad, India

Diet And Aggression

An Intimate Relationship

What's the relationship between diet and aggression? Would people be less violent places if they ate less meat? Or are there other nutritional changes that could influence an offender's behavior for the better?

It's not hard to find claims that 'meat eating promotes more aggressive behavior - a lack of gentleness in personality, and arrogance.' Another common argument on the topic is that "in nature carnivorous animals are fierce and aggressive, while non-carnivorous ones are peaceful and sociable."

The idea that meat promotes aggression can be traced in Western thought. Plutarch argued there is an

> *"Wars will never cease while men still kill other animals for food, for to turn any living creature into a roast, a steak, a chop, or any other type of 'meat' takes the same kind of violence, the same kind of bloodshed, and the same kind of mental processes required to change a living man into a dead soldier."*
>
> *~ Agnes Ryan, For the Church Door*

explicit trajectory from meat-eating to war and murder: "at the beginning it was some wild and harmful animal that was eaten, then a bird or fish that had its flesh torn. And so when our murderous instincts had tasted blood and grew practised on wild animals, they advanced to the labouring ox and the well-behaved sheep and the housewarding cock; thus, little by little giving a hard edge to our insatiable appetite, we have advanced to wars and the slaughter and murder of human beings."

A much-cited quote attributed to the mathematician Pythagoras made the same claim: "For as long as men massacre animals, they will kill each other. Indeed, he who sows the seed of murder and pain cannot reap joy and love."

And there are plenty of modern folk who believe there's a link between meat eating and aggression. Lance Armstrong's LiveStrong website suggests that, "People who rely on sugar and high-fat foods such as meat are more prone to violence and depression."

Eating meat (at times to the exclusion of other nutrients) may lead to behavior changes. According to Dr. John Briffa, a medical doctor who leans toward a holistic approach to healthcare, mood and behavior are directly related to the food you eat. People who rely on sugar and high-fat foods such as meat are more prone to violence and depression. The nutrients found in fruits, vegetables and whole grains are vital to maintaining a healthy emotional balance. Mood swings are more easily controlled as well when you eat a balanced diet of fat, protein and carbohydrates.

When you eat a meal high in carbohydrates, your brain releases tryptophan, which is a calming agent that helps you sleep. The amino acids found in meat, on the other hand, encourage production of tyrosine, according to the Franklin Institute. Tyrosine in the body produces dopamine and norepinephrine production in the brain. As a result, you feel more energetic and alert. Dopamine helps you to remain motivated about the challenges in your day and to maintain assertiveness.

Also, meat contains high amounts of adrenaline, due to the terrifying experience the animals undergo in the slaughterhouse. The high levels of adrenaline contained in meat makes the consumer aggressive, anxious and exhausts the human adrenal glands, which over time, leads to hypertension.

Consequences of Meat Protein on Human Behaviour

Animal proteins listed on labels as "meat" come from the muscular tissue of land-based vertebrates, whose carcasses are used by human beings for food. To be specific, the animals are: cattle (oxen, buffalo, bison); deer (including roebucks, fallow deer, reindeer); camels, elks, dromedaries; goats, sheep; donkeys, horses; hares, rabbits; hedgehogs, hippopotamuses, kangaroos; and swine (pigs, wild boars).

"I expect after you have many times seen a deer or woodchuck blown to bits, the thought of a human being blown to bits is that much less impossible to conceive."

~ *Medieval scholar Grace Knole in The James Joyce Murderss*

Humans also eat the flesh of marine vertebrates: fish and other aquatic animals (whales, frogs). And there is also meat from different types of birds (poultry, ducks, turkeys, ostriches, various gamebirds). Even invertebrates such as octopuses, lobsters, prawns, squids and snails are welcome as food.

All these proteins taken from the animal world means an absolute bloodbath, and it is not only unnecessary and morally repugnant, but also responsible for physical diseases brought on by toxaemia, even including cancer, and psychological disorders brought on by the tendency towards aggression. What we understand by the word "meat" are mostly muscle tissues containing saturated fats, which are injurious to human health.

Meateaters also eat liver, pancreas, thymus, saliva glands, kidney or brain - organs not made up of muscle tissues; additionally meateaters eat tripe, which is part of the complex stomach of ruminants; also many types of sausages, such as cooked pressed pork, spiced pork, baloney, ham, salami, frankfurters, stuffed pig's trotters, and so on.

And meateaters eat tongue or bovine tail muscles, or sausage or dried salted beef or bacon, and so on, not to mention caviar, mullet roe, or, as in China, dogmeat, or offal or calf's intestines.

Eating such enormous quantities of animal proteins has a profound effect on human behaviour. Generally in nature carnivorous animals are fierce and aggressive, while non-carnivorous ones are peaceful and sociable. Another thing that can easily be seen is the gradual reduction in aggression in human beings as they move from a diet containing large amounts of meat towards one excluding high protein foods, especially meat.

It is also well known that dogs, although carnivorous in nature, keep guard and attack strangers more effectively if they are fed larger than normal meat rations. Similarly, in wartime, when men are to take part in highly risky military action, they have to be given larger meat rations. Here meat is used as a drug to develop aggression, violence and moral insensitivity.

In Homer's Iliad, for example, the warriors have meat-based banquets between one battle and the next. Seneca used to point out that among the big meateaters you could find tyrants, organisers of massacres, feuds and fratricidal wars, instigators of murder, slave-traders, while those who fed on the fruits of the earth behaved gently. Liebig tells how the bear in Giesen zoo became extremely restless and dangerous if forced to eat meat instead of vegetable food.

The slogan "meat means energy" is used by those who want to justify meat eating, because this society, based on free and unfettered competition and social climbing, demands we wear an aggressive scowl which will help us get on in the world, win our life struggles.

These brief sociobiological references already allow us to state with certainty that meat has a negative effect on human behaviour. We can say this because, as everyone can see, human beings are readily influenced by environmental factors, especially diet, an important truth encapsulated by the great Ludwig Feuerbach way back in 1855, when he famously said, "Der Mann ist vas er isst." ("Man is what he eats.") But, more than a century earlier, in 1728, a distinguished Italian expert, Bartolomeo Beccari (doctor, chemist, and chemistry teacher at Bologna University) delivered the judgement, "Quid alius sumus, nisi it unde alimur?" ("What else are we, if not what we eat?") so expressing what Feuerbach would say much later.

It was not by chance that both these great thinkers were vegetarians. Beccari, among other things, discovered gluten and isovalencies between animal and vegetable proteins. Man is not just an alimentary canal to fill with various foods, but a thinking being whose brain, like any other part of the body, must be nourished with the material necessary for its metabolism that is delivered by the blood stream.

A Healthy Mind Stays In A Healthy Body

And since most of the food we eat is produced by a food industry concerned only with profit, without regard for our real dietary needs, the so called science of nutrition is manipulated by this chemicalised industry. Pharmaceutical industry works in collusion with the food industry. One makes us sick and then the other comes along, pretending to cure us. But both the industries are concerned with our pockets, not us.

Mainstay of this food industry are junk foods, especially those based on meat proteins, which they sell with the powerful assistance of the media. Widespread popularity of such 'foods' is responsible for the proliferation of violence in every nook and corner of the world.

This food culture is responsible for what UN calls 'a tsunami of diseases' sweeping the world. And we all know the saying, 'Mens sana in corpore sano', a healthy mind in a healthy body. When the body is diseased, so would be the mind. A sick mind stays in a sick body.

Bodily health can not be neglected if we want social sanity. In the 17th century, the British philosopher, John Locke, in his work Some

> "Is it not a reproach that man is a carnivorous animal? True, he can and does live, in a great measure, by preying on other animals; but this is a miserable way--as any one who will go to snaring rabbits, or slaughtering lambs, may learn--and he will be regarded as a benefactor of his race who shall teach man to confine himself to a more innocent and wholesome diet. What my own practice may be, I have no doubt that it is a part of the destiny of the human race, in its gradual improvement, to leave off eating animals, as surely as the savage tribes have left off eating each other when they came in contact with the more civilized."
> ~ Henry David Thoreau in "Walden"

Thoughts Concerning Education (1693), stressed the validity of this saying about the health of the mind depending on that of the body.

In this context we can see the great importance of vegetarianism, which detoxifies the body and purifies the blood supply to the brain. Consequently it promotes the auspicious qualities of self-control, tolerance, gentleness, love, sociability and sharing in masses.

Electrical activity in the brain as shown by EEGs has shown that the vegetarian diet induces alpha waves, which indicate a state of neuromuscular relaxation not just of the brain but of the whole body. It's no wonder that since time immemorial, hermits and sages have preferred a plant based diet and through the centuries the most intelligent, the most cultured, the most open, the most tolerant people in the world have been vegetarians, in all fields of knowledge: in science, philosophy, art, literature, medicine, and so on.

A Tool of Mind Control And Manipulation

When meat is ingested, the blood supply to the brain carries the meat catabolites with it and affects the brain's physiology. This promotes negative qualities like intolerance, quarrelsomeness, aggression, hatred and antisocial behaviour.

Those in power know how to use the weapon of food to influence human behaviour towards what is most convenient

"For hundreds of thousands of years the stew in the pot has brewed hatred and resentment that is difficult to stop. If you wish to know why there are disasters of armies and weapons in the world, listen to the piteous cries from the slaughterhouse at midnight."
Ancient Chinese verse

for their agenda, and so they do all they can to encourage us to eat dead, poisoned, intoxicating foods like meat. Ultimately the target is the brain, which they want to render incapable of understanding and analyzing.

In conclusion, while vegetarianism favours the highest cognitive faculties, carcasses depress them, encouraging behaviours damaging to the individual and society, and reduce serotonin levels. A meal high in meat proteins reduces tryptophane levels in the brain, and leads to aggression and anxiety. The more we rely on the fruits of the earth and follow vegetarian principles, the more positive our behaviour becomes. Our choice of food influences our behaviour and emotions.

This is what Dr Rossi says, and its experimental confirmation has come from John Fernstrom and Richard Hurthman, biologists in the Department of Nutrition and Dietary Sciences at the Massachusetts Institute of Technology.

"Watch out for him - he bites."

Some 'nutritionists' against vegetarianism maintain that aggression is not caused by meat proteins, but rather it is an innate human trait.

The wellknown anthropologist, Luigi Lombardi Satriani says that it is just an excuse for us to blame aggression on nature, an excuse we as a society use to escape our responsibilities. If aggression is innate, violence would be a universal phenomena which anthropology shows to be wrong.

Non-violent cultures have existed and still do. India for example, has no record of it ever invading another country and it is largely vegetarian. There are certain tribes in Africa or groups of Indians in north-west Brazil or the Piaroa Indians in Venezuela who have built peaceful societies, based on cooperation and without a trace of aggression. Hatred is unknown in these societies and these people are largely vegetarians. No traditional society ate meat like we do today.

Meat Is Born of Violence And Brute Force

Meat eating requires an earlier act of violence, the killing of an animal.

Meat eating, based on murder as it is, is inevitably associated with violence and brute force, whereas vegetarianism is based on the stability, tranquillity and serenity of the vegetable world which in its nobility draws life and strength from mother earth.

According to professor Carlo Sirtori, a distinguished clinician and scientist, meat eating leads to aggression because phosphorus and calcium are to be found in meat in a ratio of 50:1. Meat eating leads to elevated and unnatural levels of phosphorus in humans, whose milk has a 1:2 phosphorus-calcium ratio. According to him, lower calcium levels lead to irritable and aggressive behaviour and sometimes convulsions in small children.

During the Gulf War in 1992, US marines getting ready for action were supplied with 50,000 turkeys in addition to the normal meat rations. The reason: "They are soldiers and have to eat a lot of meat." We can conclude by quoting the words of the philosopher, Jacopo Moleschott, "As long as the Irishman is fed with potatoes, he will be subjugated by the Englishman eating steak and roast beef."

Source:

Armando D'Elia, President, AVI Scientific Committee

Translations by Hugh Rees, Milan, Associazione Vegetariana Italiana (AVI), 6th European Vegetarian Congress, Bussolengo, Italy, September 1997

Cordain, Loren (2007). "Implications of Plio-pleistocene diets for modern humans".

Milton, Katharine, "A hypothesis to explain the role of meat-eating in human evolution",Evolutionary Anthropology: Issues, News, and Reviews Volume 8, Issue 1, 1999

Craig WJ, Mangels AR (2009). "Position of the American Dietetic Association: vegetarian diets"

David Benatar (2001). "Why the Naive Argument against Moral Vegetarianism Really is Naive".

"Animals and Ethics [Internet Encyclopedia of Philosophy]". Iep.utm.edu. January 13, 2010.

Erik Marcus (2000). Vegan: The New Ethics of Eating

Kochhal, M. (October 2004). "Vegetarianism: jainism and vegetarianism (ahisma)".

Teachings on Love, Thich Nhat Hanh, Berkley, Parallax Press, 1998.

Al-Qaeda Militant

Says No to Vegetarian Food

Al-Qaeda militant Ghulam Rasool Khan alias Khan Mirza, who was formally arrested in Purnia in Bihar while trying to cross over to Bangladesh in January 2010, put forward an unusual demand.

"Provide me two kg of mutton and one kg of chicken daily or else I will sit on hunger strike inside Purnia jail", the militant informed the jail authorities.

Jail authorities said Mirza refused to take vegetarian food served to him for two days after he was lodged in the jail, saying he was a habitual meat eater.

I happen to notice that those people who eat a lot of meat tend to be more violent. Meanwhile, vegans and vegetarians are more pacific. Is their temperament the result of their diets, or does their temperament influence the diets they choose? Perhaps compassionate people are more open to the idea of a vegetarian diet. I believe in some cases that could be true, but in my case I noticed that I've become less aggressive.

~ Sarah Dean, Sydney

Confirming this, IG (Prisons), D Kumar said "We will, like other prisoners, serve meal to the prisoner in keeping with the jail manual...But, at the same time, we will abide by any court directive in this regard".

Reference
Staff Writer, Press Trust of India (PTI), 23 Jan 2010
DNA India, Saturday, 23 January 2010

Although Jada Bharata was forced to carry the palanquin, he did not give up his sympathetic feelings toward the poor ants passing on the road. A devotee of the Lord does not forget his devotional service and other favorable activities, even when he is in a most distressful condition. While walking on the road, he could not forget his duty to avoid killing even an ant. A Vaisnava is never envious or unnecessarily violent. There were many ants on the path, but Jada Bharata took care by looking ahead three feet. When the ants were no longer in his way, he would place his foot on the ground. A Vaisnava is always very kind at heart to all living entities.
—*Srila Prabhupada (Srimad Bhagavatam 5.10.2)*

Food

Directly Affects Brain And Its Behavior

We live in violent times. Americans are seven times more likely to die of homicide and twenty times more likely to die from shooting than people in other developed countries.[1] Between 1984 and 1994, the number of young murderers under age eighteen in the U.S. increased threefold.[2-4]

In the 1990s, a new form of deadly violence raised its head in America. The first mass school slaying occurred in 1992 when Wayne Lo killed a student and a professor at a remote school in Massachusetts. This act set the stage for an escalating pattern of chilling destruction aimed at students and carried out by students,

There are studies that demonstrate that taking steroids ups aggressive and violent behavior, and in some cases animals are even given steroids directly, which comes through in their flesh. Even if they aren't given steroids their animal (natural) hormones may act very much like steroids in the human body after we consume their muscle and fat tissues.

However, there's another explanation for someone getting cranky and mean on Atkins – the diet actually is destroying your internal organs, so someone on the diet is literally sick. We all know people who get impossible to be around when they have a cold, so imagine how they act when their livers and kidneys are being driven toward failure.

~ John Hall, October 17, 2008

violence that increases every year. From the 1999 Columbine shootings in Colorado to the recent shootings in Newtown, Connecticut, Americans are desperately searching for answers.

In his book Confronting Violence: Answers to Questions About the Epidemic Destroying America's Homes and Communities, George Gellert, MD, discusses "tested strategies to prevent violent

WHEN YOU EAT MEAT...
YOU EAT THE PAIN
YOU EAT THE TRAUMA
YOU EAT THE SLAIN
YOU EAT THE HORROR
YOU EAT THE STRESS
YOU EAT THE MURDER
YOU EAT THE MESS
YOU EAT THE VOICELESS
YOU EAT THE CAGED
YOU EAT THE HELPLESS
YOU EAT THE RAGED
YOU EAT THE CAPTURED
YOU EAT THE MEEK
YOU EAT THE TERROR
YOU EAT THE REEK
YOU EAT THE BLOOD
YOU EAT THE GORE...
AND THEN YOU WONDER
WHY THERE'S WAR

crime" without providing any evidence that any of these strategies—electronic tracking, hotlines, education and training have actually worked. In fact, it is obvious that they have not.[5]

The disturbing tendencies we see today contrast strongly with Dr. Weston Price's descriptions of harmonious, well-nourished primitive cultures—from smiling, joyful South Sea Islanders to highly spiritual Gaelic fisherfolk to Swiss villagers celebrating "one for all and all for one" during their summer festivals.[6] Likewise, Dr. Francis Pottenger described peaceful, harmonious behavior among well-nourished cats. Both cats and humans degenerated into disharmonious behavior patterns with the change to foods devitalized by heat and processing.[7]

" HAVE YOU EVER CONSIDERED SEEING A DOCTOR ABOUT YOUR AGGRESSION ISSUES? "

Modern commentators are blind to the solution, a solution that is in plain sight: clearly defining good nutrition and putting it back into the mouths of our children, starting before they are even conceived. . . because food is information and that information directly affects the emotions, the nervous system, the brain and behavior.

Source

Sylvia Onusic, April 22, 2013

1. Woolf SH and Laudan A, Editors; U.S. Health in International Perspective: Shorter Lives, Poorer Health. National Research Council; Institute of Medicine. 2013. The National Academies Press.Washington DC.

2. Perry, BD, Aggression and Violence: The Neurobiology of Experience. Teachers.

3. Gardner, A. Americans Suffer Worse Health Than Peers in Other Countries. March 8, 2013. Health Day.

4. Mercola. J. Americans are Less Healthy and Die Sooner Than People in Other Developed Nations January 23, 2013.

5. Gellert GA. Confronting Violence. Boulder:Westview Press,1997, 2012.

6. Price, WA. Nutrition and Physical Degeneration, La Mesa: Price-Pottenger Nutrition Foundation, 2008.

7. Pottenger FM, Jr. Edited by Pottenger E & Pottenger, RT, Jr. Pottenger's Cats. A Study in Nutrition, La Mesa: Price-Pottenger Nutrition Foundation. La Mesa, 1983.

4

A Jounrey From Chicago Stockyards to Auschwitz Death Camps

Laying The Foundation For The World Wars

Where does all the war, racism, terrorism, violence, and cruelty that's so endemic to human civilization come from? Why do humans exploit and massacre each other so regularly? Why is our species so violence-prone? To answer these questions we would do well to think about our exploitation and slaughter of animals and its effect on human civilization. Could it be that we oppress and kill each other so readily because our abuse and slaughter of animals has desensitized us to the suffering and death of others?

In 1917 Sigmund Freud put the issue in perspective when he wrote:

"In the course of his development towards culture man acquired a dominating position over his fellow-creatures in the animal kingdom. Not content with this supremacy, however, he began to place a gulf between his nature and theirs. He denied the possession of reason to them, and to himself he attributed an immortal soul, and made claims to a divine descent which permitted him to annihilate the bond of community between him and the animal kingdom."

The domination, control, and manipulation that characterizes the way humans treat animals who come under their control has set the tone and served as a model for the way humans treat each other. It also led humans to place other humans--captives, enemies, strangers, and those who were different or disliked--on the other side of the great divide where they were vilified as "beasts," "pigs," "dogs," "monkeys," "rats," and "vermin."

Designating other people as animals has always been an ominous development because it sets them up for humiliation, exploitation, and murder. As Leo Kuper writes in Genocide: Its Political Use in the Twentieth Century, "the animal world has been a particularly fertile source of metaphors of dehumanization."

Animal Slaughter And Holocaust

Animal exploitation and the Holocaust have a direct connection. Take the case of Henry Ford, whose impact on the twentieth century began, metaphorically speaking, at an American slaughterhouse and ended at Auschwitz.

In his autobiography, My Life and Work (1922), Ford revealed that his inspiration for assembly-line production came from a visit he made as a young man to a Chicago slaughterhouse.

"I believe that this was the first moving line ever installed. The idea [of the assembly line] came in a general way from the overhead trolley that the Chicago packers use in dressing beef."

A Swift and Company publication from that time described the division-of-labor principle that so impressed Ford: "The slaughtered animals, suspended head downward from a moving chain, or conveyor, pass from workman to workman, each of whom performs some particular step in the process."

It was but one step from the industrialized slaughter of animals to the assembly-line mass murder of people. In J. M. Coetzee's novel, The Lives of Animals, the protagonist Elizabeth Costello tells her audience:

"Chicago showed us the way; it was from the Chicago stockyards that the Nazis learned how to process bodies."

Most people are not aware of the central role of the slaughterhouse in the history of American industry. "Historians have deprived the packers of their rightful title of mass-production pioneers," writes James Barrett in his study of Chicago's packinghouse workers in the early 1900s, "for it was not Henry Ford but Gustavus Swift and Philip Armour who developed the assembly-line technique that continues to symbolize the rationalized organization of work."

Henry Ford, who was so impressed by the efficient way meat packers slaughtered and dismantled animals in Chicago, made his own unique contribution to the slaughter of people in Europe. Not only did he develop the assembly-line method that Germans used to kill Jews, but he launched a vicious anti-Semitic campaign that helped make the Holocaust happen.

From Animal Breeding to Genocide

Another American contribution to Nazi Germany's Final Solution--eugenics--was rooted in animal exploitation. The breeding of domesticated animals-- breeding the most desirable and castrating and killing the rest--became the model for American and German eugenic efforts to upgrade their populations. America led the way with regard to forced sterilizations, but Nazi Germany quickly caught up and went on to euthanasia killings and genocide.

The desire to improve the hereditary qualities of the human population had had its beginnings in the 1860s when Francis Galton, an English scientist and cousin of Charles Darwin, turned from meteorology to the study of heredity (he coined the term "eugenics" in 1881). By the end of the nineteenth century, genetic theories, founded on the assumption that heredity was based on rigid genetic patterns little influenced by social environment, dominated scientific thought.

The eugenics movement in America began with the creation of the American Breeders' Association (ABA) in 1903. At the

second meeting of the ABA in 1905, a series of reports about the great success achieved in the selective breeding of animals and plants prompted delegates to ask why such techniques could not be applied to human beings. The creation of a committee on Human Heredity, or Eugenics, at the third ABA meeting in 1906 launched the American eugenics movement in America.

Its leader was poultry researcher Charles B. Davenport, who served as the director of the Eugenics Record Office (ERO), who described eugenics as "the science of the improvement of the human race by better breeding," looked forward to the time when a woman would no more accept a man "without knowing his biologico-genealogical history" than a stockbreeder would take "a sire for his colts or calves who was without pedigree."

He believed that "the most progressive revolution in history" could be achieved if "human matings could be placed upon the same high plane as that of horse breeding."

Animal Sterilization - Applied To Humans

Sterilization began in America in 1887, when the superintendent of the Cincinnati Sanitarium published the first public recommendation for the sterilization of criminals, both as a punishment and a way to prevent further crime.

Authorities used the same method to sterilize male criminals that farmers used on their male animals not selected for breeding--castration. Castration was the preferred method used to sterilize male criminal offenders until 1899, when vasectomy was adopted because it was more practical.

By the 1930s compulsory sterilization had widespread support in the United States, with college presidents, clergymen, mental health workers, and school principals among its strongest supporters.

The United States quickly became the model for other countries that wanted to sterilize their "defectives." Denmark was the first European country to pass such a law in 1929, followed in rapid succession by other European nations.

In Germany, which passed its sterilization law six months after the Nazis came to power, eugenics established deep roots in medical and scientific circles after World War I.

Life Unworthy of Life

In 1920 two respected academics--Karl Binding, a widely published legal scholar, and Alfred Hoche, a professor of psychiatry with a specialty in neuropathology--publishedDie Freigabe der Vernichtung lebensunwerten Lebens (Authorization for the Destruction of Life Unworthy of Life).

In it they argued that German law should permit the mercy killing of institutionalized patients who werelebensunwert ("unworthy of life") and whose lives were "without purpose" and a burden to their relatives and society.

Beginning in the 1920s, the Rockefeller Foundation and other American foundations provided extensive financial support for eugenics research in Germany. By the time the Nazis came to power, more than twenty institutes for "racial hygiene" had already been established at German universities.

The Law on Preventing Hereditarily Ill Progeny, which the Nazi government issued on July 14, 1933, required the sterilization of patients suffering from mental and physical disorders in state hospitals and nursing homes.

By then, the United States had already sterilized more than 15,000 people, most of them while they were incarcerated in prisons or homes for the mentally ill. America's sterilization laws made such a favorable impression on Hitler and his followers that Nazi Germany looked to the United States for racial leadership.

Hitler took a special interest in the progress of eugenics in the United States. "I have studied with great interest the laws of several American states concerning prevention of reproduction by people whose progeny would, in all probability, be of no value or be injurious to the racial stock."

Nazi Germany Overtakes United States

However, Nazi Germany's sterilization efforts quickly surpassed those of the United States. Estimates of the total number of Germans sterilized under the Nazis range from 300,000 to 400,000.

The Germans were also impressed by America's immigration laws, which barred people with hereditary diseases and limited people from non-Nordic countries. In 1934 the German race anthropologist Hans F. K. Gunther told an audience at the

University of Munich that American immigration laws should serve as a guideline and inspiration for Nazi Germany. German race scientists also admired America's segregation and miscegenation laws.

In fact, Nazi theorists complained that German race policies lagged behind America's, pointing out that in certain southern states a person with 1/32 black ancestry was legally black, while in Germany, if somebody was 1/8 Jewish or in many instances 1/4 Jewish, that person was considered legally Aryan.

Americans were the strongest foreign supporters of Nazi race policies. In 1934 Eugenic News proclaimed that in "no country of the world is eugenics more active as an applied science than in Germany" and praised the Nazi sterilization law as an historic advance.

Scores of American anthropologists, psychologists, psychiatrists, and geneticists visited Nazi Germany where they had high-level meetings with Nazi leaders and scientists and visited racial hygiene institutes, public health departments, and hereditary health courts.

When the Americans returned and reported on their visits in professional journals and newsletters, they lauded the German sterilization program.

An Animal Beginning

Like the American Charles Davenport, Heinrich Himmler, head of the Nazi SS and a main architect of the Final Solution, began his eugenics education with animal breeding. His agricultural studies and experience breeding chickens convinced him that since all behavioral characteristics are hereditary, the most effective way to shape the future of a population--human or otherwise--was to institute breeding projects that favored the desirable and eliminated the undesirable.

Himmler was soon in a position to apply eugenic principles and methods to human beings in a way no American eugenicist was ever able to do.

Auschwitz - The Largest Human Slaughterhouse Ever

Rudolf Hoss, the commandant of Auschwitz and another strong supporter of eugenics with a farming background, wrote in his autobiography after the war that the original plan for Auschwitz

Just like one has committed murder, so by law he must be hanged. By law. That is the general law everywhere, all over the world: life for life. So similarly, in the God's law there is no such thing that if you kill a human being you'll be killed, and if you kill an animal you won't be killed. That is imperfect law, man-made law. Therefore Jesus Christ said, "Thou shall not kill." No question of... They have modified, "This killing means murdering." Christ does not say. What is your proof that if you committed mistake, a mistake, instead of writing "Thou shall not commit murder," here is written, "Thou shall not kill," general. Otherwise Christ has no intelligence. He cannot use the proper word. But you are misusing the order of Lord Christ.

So you are suffering. You are maintaining so many slaughterhouses, and when it will be mature, there will be war, the wholesale murder. Finished. One atom bomb — finished. You'll have to suffer. Don't think that "Innocent animals, they cannot protest. Let us kill and eat." No. You'll be also punished. Wait for accumulation of your sinful activities, and there will be war, and the America will drop the atom bomb, and Russia will be finished. Both will be finished. Go on now enjoying. It takes time. Just like even if you infect some disease, it takes time. Not that immediately you infect, and immediately the disease is there. No. It takes a week's time or so. What is called? A quarantine, quarantine...

Devotee: Period of incubation.

—Srila Prabhupada (Lecture, Srimad-Bhagavatam 6.1.32, Honolulu, May 31, 1976)

had been to make it into a major agricultural research station. "All kinds of stockbreeding was to be pursued there."

However, in the summer of 1941 Himmler summoned him to Berlin to inform him of the fateful order for the mass extermination of the Jews of Europe, an order that soon turned Auschwitz into "the largest human slaughterhouse that history had ever known."

By the summer of 1942 Auschwitz was a vast, full-service eugenics center for the improvement of animal and human populations, complete with stockbreeding centers and the Birkenau extermination camp for the culling of Jews, Gypsies, and other "sub-humans."

Correcting The "Nature's Mistakes"

Germany's eugenics campaign entered a new, deadly phase in 1939 when Hitler issued a secret order for the systematic murder of mentally retarded, emotionally disturbed, and physically infirm

What Came Before:

"I have a tough stomach, and I've put myself through a lot," explains Steve-O. "But when I first found out what happens to animals on modern factory farms and in today's slaughterhouses, I wanted to throw up -- I literally couldn't believe it. I narrated this short film for Farm Sanctuary because I'm committed to doing what I can to show people all the disgusting things that happen to farm animals, and to encourage everyone to make more compassionate choices. I love that when someone does a Google search for 'Steve-O explicit video,' they're going to find 'What Came Before.' I hope a lot of them go vegetarian."

Germans who were an embarrassment to the myth of Aryan supremacy.

Once "defective" children were identified and institutionalized, doctors and nurses either starved them to death, or gave them lethal doses of luminal (a sedative), veronal (sleeping pills), morphine, or scopolamine. The "euthanasia" program--named Operation T4, or simply T4-- transported adults to special killing centers outfitted with gas chambers. T4 killed between 70,000 and 90,000 Germans before it was officially stopped in August 1941. In 1942, not long after German psychiatrists had sent the last of their patients to the gas chambers, the Journal of the American Psychiatric Association published an article that called for the killing of retarded children ("nature's mistakes").

Slaughterhouse Experience Comes Handy

The breeding and culling of animals that was at the center of American and German eugenics produced a number of key T4 personnel, including those sent to Poland to operate the death camps.

Victor Brack, T4's chief manager, received a diploma in agriculture from the Technical University in Munich, while Hans Hefelmann, who headed the office that coordinated the killing of handicapped children, had a

"... he had made of this fair earth, if not a heaven for man, at least a hell for animals."
(Lewis Carroll, 1832-1898)

doctorate in agricultural economics. Before spending more than two years at the Hartheim euthanasia center in Austria, Bruno Bruckner had worked as a porter in a Linz slaughterhouse.

Willi Mentz, an especially sadistic guard at Treblinka, had been in charge of cows and pigs at two T4 killing centers, Grafeneck and Hadamar. Treblinka's last commandant, Kurt Franz, trained with a master butcher before joining the SS. Karl Frenzel, who worked as a stoker at Hadamar before being posted to the Sobibor death camp, had also been a butcher.

For German personnel sent to Poland to exterminate Jews, experience in the exploitation and slaughter of animals proved to be excellent training.

Slaughter of Animals And Mass Murder of People

The exploitation and slaughter of animals provides the precedent for the mass murder of people and makes it more likely because it conditions us to withhold empathy, compassion, and respect from others who are different.

Isaac Bashevis Singer wrote, "There is only one little step from killing animals to creating gas chambers a la Hitler." Indeed there is.

About the same time the German Jewish philosopher Theodor Adorno made a similar point: "Auschwitz begins whenever someone looks at a slaughterhouse and thinks: they're only animals." Indeed it does.

Source

Charles Patterson, Anti-Semitism: The Road to the Holocaust and Beyond

Charles Patterson, Eternal Treblinka: Our Treatment of Animals and the Holocaust.

"Holocaust Map of Concentration and Death Camps", History1900s, 16 June 2010.

5

Slaughter Houses And Increased Crime Rates

By Maneka Gandhi

When my father was posted as an army officer to Bangalore, we lived on Pottery Road near a large slaughterhouse . The smell was infernal. There were fights all the time. We moved very quickly and for many years I completely blocked it from my memory.

A famous Indian monk went to America and as he neared Chicago, he is said to have seen a large black miasma over the city. It was then the largest stockyard and slaughterhouse in the country. It was also the main centre of crime and run by gangs.

Which are some of the most dangerous cities in India? I would put Rampur in Uttar Pradesh on the top of my list. The police and armed forces are wary of it too. Recently, a full scale attack by terrorists on a para military division took place there. Murders and other forms of violent crime are common. It also has the last number of illegal slaughterhouses killing cows and buffaloes by the thousands every day. Then there is Mewat region in Haryana where even police officers refuse to go. It is the largest centre for illegal slaughter in North India, and a hub for the wildlife trade as well.

In Delhi one such dangerous place is the walled city near Jama Masjid. Here you can see dead cows being skinned in every lane.

Which is the most dangerous part of your city ? Is it not the area around slaughterhouses?

Every one knows instinctively that anyone who can kill an animal with impunity can kill a fellow human being just as easily.

In Bareilly recently, A Superintendant of Police tried to stop a truck carrying cows to Rampur . The crew on the truck whipped out guns and shot him. This is not an unusual occurrence. Every overloaded slaughter truck carries guns. Many of my activists have been shot at. Before shooting, the first attempt of the driver is to run you over with his vehicle.

In 2009, an interesting study was published after 9 years of research: Slaughterhouses and Increased Crime Rates: An Empirical Analysis of the Spillover From "The Jungle" Into the Surrounding Community by Amy J. Fitzgerald, University of Windsor , Linda Kalof, Michigan State University, and Thomas Dietz, Michigan State University.

One hundred years ago, the famous author Upton Sinclair wrote a book called The Jungle. This book details the working and living conditions of workers in and around the stockyard slaughterhouses

We also need to be mindful of our behaviors as well. A lot of vegan women have told me similar stories, where their vegan male partners shoved them or slapped them during an argument or even of sexual assault occurring in groups of activists. This is rare and by and large I think vegetarians are more peaceful and compassionate percentage-wise than the general population. So, in short, yes I think there are chemical reasons that a meat-heavy diet might make someone more aggressive.

~ Paul Thompson, Cambridge MA

in Chicago. In explaining the numerous fights instigated by slaughterhouse workers after working hours, Sinclair noted a connection between these fights and the killing and dismembering of animals all day at work.

According to Sinclair, "these two-o'clock-in- the-morning fights, are like a forest fire.. men who have to crack the heads of animals all day seem to get into the habit, and practice on their friends, and even on their families, between times." The book denounced the massive slaughterhouse complex in Chicago as a "jungle," and said that all crime and criminals in America were born out of this slaughterhouse culture.

The purpose of this study was to prove/disprove the Sinclair contention. The authors write : "Contemporary studies conducted by social scientists documenting the negative effects of slaughterhouses on communities have not attended to the possibility (which Sinclair alludes to) that the type of work undertaken in slaughterhouses is a contributing factor to increased crime rates in slaughterhouse communities.

The meatpacking industry's effect on physical environment and human health and on the high rate of injuries to workers has been carefully documented by scholars. This study analyzes population/jobs/crime data of 1994-2002 in 581 nonmetropolitan counties to analyze the effect of slaughterhouses on the surrounding communities .

The findings indicate that slaughterhouse employment increases total arrest rates, arrests for violent crimes, rape, other sex offenses, vandalism, arson, robbery, assault and disorderly conduct in comparison with other industries. Research demonstrates that in communities where slaughterhouses operate, there is an increase in crime.

For instance, documented crime increases include a 130% increase in violent crimes in Finney County, Kansas and a 63% increase in Lexington, Nebraska. The Canadian town of Brooks, Alberta witnessed a 70% increase in reported crime. Particularly telling is the fact that the arrests in counties with 7,500 slaughterhouse employees are more than double than in those where there are no slaughterhouse employees. This proves the existence of a "Sinclair effect" unique to the violent workplace of the slaughterhouse, a factor ignored previously in the sociology of violence.

Various explanations for these increases in crime have been proposed. The objective of this study was (1) to test the theories that explain the crime increases and (2) to compare the effects of slaughterhouse employment on crime rates to the effects of similar industries, to see if the effects of slaughterhouses are unique.

These were the theories that existed and this is what they found:

a. "The workers were mainly immigrants and more likely to be involved in criminal activities." A link between immigrant populations and crime rates, however, has not been found. On the contrary, studies have found that typical immigration does not result in crime increases.

b. "The much increased violence in these communities is not because of the slaughterhouses but because the workers are lower middle class, usually uneducated hard drinking people who are mainly young males." Studies have found that age does not have

You have 35 seconds: Gut the cow without damaging its organs, and be sure not to drop the stomach on the floor. Do not cut yourself with the swift-moving blade; do not touch the scalding sanitary surfaces. Then, walk in hot water to clean your white rubber boots. Swap your knife out and start over again. Again and again.
~ Daniel Piotrowski, A former slaughterman

a significant effect on some types of crimes, such as burglary and homicide

c. "Crime increases are the result of population booms and social disorganization." In simple terms that means that the population is poor with a great tendency to shift jobs and migrate both in and out of the towns resulting in social disorganization and consequent increases in crime. But these explanations do not hold water because people in identical low paid, filthy, dangerous, blue collar towns with high unemployment and heavy alcohol habits have not got the same spike in violence.

The study took similar towns with comparative industries : "Iron and steel forging, truck trailer manufacturing, motor vehicle metal stamping, sign manufacturing, and industrial laundering. These industries are categorized as manufacturing, have high immigrant worker concentrations, low pay, routinized labor, repetitive, and dangerous conditions. These were not associated with a rise in crime at all. In fact crime rates were on their way down. No connection was found between high unemployment rates and violent crime.

The researchers concluded that : "the industrialization of slaughter has the strongest adverse effects". The unique work of killing and dismembering animals in slaughterhouses has resulted in the types of crime which Upton Sinclair referred to as 'the jungle' in the community.

Fitzgerald says at the end "We believe that this is another of a growing list of social problems that need explicit attention ."

The findings seem so obvious to me: When a person removes a non-human animal from moral consideration, he removes humans from moral consideration as well. This is seen in historical examples where colonialism or genocide used the idea of the victims as 'animals' to justify murder or oppression.

Someone who has the ability to rip thousands of animals throats is not a gentle and law abiding person. People who have made documentaries about slaughterhouses show workers kicking animals, playing football with chickens, throwing cow eyeballs at each other, urinating on bodies and masturbating on dying animals, a state of desensitization so extreme that it could only spill over as general violence.

Industrialization of slaughter has instituted a killing culture of in the human society. We are ready to wreak havoc on each other just as easily we do so on the animals. Each war is surpassing the previous one in terms of brutality. The news of thousands dying no longer shock us anymore.

While killing an animal, we kill the better part of ourselves, and pay the price in the form of wars, crime, obesity and poor health.

Go to a large slaughterhouse in your town. The terrifying experience will be enough to make you cry and vomit and taint your soul for a long time.

Suppose all the abbatoirs are changed into soybean processing plants. Doesn't even thinking about it make you feel better?

(To join Menaka Gandhi's animal welfare movement contact gandhim@nic.in)

6

Globe Witnessing "Piecemeal World War Three" - Pope

Number of war refugees exceeded 50 million for the first time since WWII - UN

Peace Is Today Dangerously In Deficit, UN High Commissioner

Pope Francis says the spate of conflicts around the globe today are effectively a "piecemeal" Third World War, condemning the arms trade and "plotters of terrorism" sowing death and destruction.

"Humanity needs to weep and this is the time to weep," Francis said in the homily of a Mass in September 2014 during a visit to Italy's largest war memorial, a large, Fascist-era monument where more than 100,000 soldiers who died in World War One are buried.

The pope began his brief visit to northern Italy by first praying in a nearby, separate cemetery for some 15,000 soldiers from five nations of the Austro-Hungarian empire which were on the losing side of the Great War that broke out 100 years ago.

"War is madness," he said in his homily before the massive, sloping granite memorial. "Even today, after the second failure of

"We pray on Sundays that we may have light
To guide our footsteps on the path we tread;
We are sick of war, we don't want to fight,
And yet we gorge ourselves upon the dead."
~ George Bernard Shaw

another world war, perhaps one can speak of a third war, one fought piecemeal, with crimes, massacres, destruction," he said.

In the past few months, Francis has made repeated appeals for an end to conflicts in Ukraine, Iraq, Syria, Gaza and parts of Africa.

"War is irrational; its only plan is to bring destruction: it seeks to grow by destroying," he said. "Greed, intolerance, the lust for power. These motives underlie the decision to go to war and they are too often justified by an ideology ...," he said.

Last month the pope, who has often condemned the concept of war in God's name, said it would be legitimate for the international community to use force to stop "unjust aggression" by Islamic State militants who have killed or displaced thousands of people in Iraq and Syria, many of them Christians.

The Long Road Home - After World War II, A Forgotten Refugee Crisis Returns

The UN refugee agency reported on World Refugee Day (June 20, 2014) that the number of refugees, asylum-seekers and internally displaced people worldwide has, for the first time in the post-World War II era, exceeded 50 million people.

UNHCR's annual Global Trends report, which is based on data compiled by governments and non-governmental partner organizations, and from the organization's own records, shows 51.2 million people were forcibly displaced at the end of 2013, fully 6 million more than the 45.2 million reported in 2012.

"Cruelty to animals is as if man did not love God."
~ Cardinal John H. Newman

By region, Asia and the Pacific had the largest refugee population overall at 3.5 million people. Sub-Saharan Africa had 2.9 million people, while the Middle East and North Africa had 2.6 million. "We are seeing here the immense costs of not ending wars, of failing to resolve or prevent conflict," said UN High Commissioner for Refugees António Guterres. "Peace is today dangerously in deficit. Humanitarians can help as a palliative, but political solutions are vitally needed. Without this, the alarming levels of conflict and the mass suffering that is reflected in these figures will continue."

The worldwide total of 51.2 million forcibly displaced represents a huge number of people in need of help, with implications both for foreign aid budgets in the world's donor nations and the absorption and hosting capacities of countries on the front lines of refugee crises.

I have been eating a lot of meat lately, and I feel like I can tear someone's head off (no joke). Here's an excerpt from a Huffington Post article:

Recent research by Arizona State University showed omnivores who went meatless felt better emotionally. Of the 39 people studied, one group kept to their omnivorous ways, a second group ate fish but no other source of animal protein, the third group ate no fish, no meat, no eggs. The first two groups reported no change in emotion or cognition. The plant-based party reported they felt more relaxed and focused than they did eating meat. I'm not saying all meat eaters are stupid. I'm saying there's a real correlation between how eating meat and feeling anger affect the body.

The Harvard School of Public Health examined 1,300 men in their 60s over the course of seven years and found the angriest guys were likelier to develop heart disease than those who could ride life's highs and lows without losing it. In another study, the Harvard School of Public Health showed eating bacon, salami, sausage, hot dogs, any meat that's been processed or cured or salted, jacks up your risk of heart disease by 42 percent and your risk of diabetes by 19 percent. Feeling anger poses a lot of the same health risks as eating meat does.

~ Hanni Gonzalez, Durban, SA, August 3, 2014

"The international community has to overcome its differences and find solutions to the conflicts of today in South Sudan, Syria, Central African Republic and elsewhere. Non-traditional donors need to step up alongside traditional donors. As many people are forcibly displaced today as the entire populations of medium-to-large countries such as Colombia or Spain, South Africa or South Korea," said Guterres.

Displacement data in the annual report covers refugees, asylum-seekers and the internally displaced. Among these, refugee numbers amounted to 16.7 million people worldwide, 11.7 million of whom are under UNHCR's care and the remainder registered with the UN Relief and Works Agency for Palestine. These totals

We want to stop these killing houses. It is very, very sinful. Therefore in Europe, so many wars. Every ten years, fifteen years, there is a big war and wholesale slaughter of the whole human kind. And these rascals, they do not see it. The reaction must be there. You are killing innocent cows and animals. Nature will take revenge. Wait for that. As soon as the time is ripe, the nature will gather all these rascals, and club, slaughter them. Finished. They will fight amongst themselves, Protestant and Catholic, Russia and France, and France and Germany. This is going on. Why? This is the nature's law. Tit for tat. You have killed. Now you get killed. Amongst yourselves. They are being sent to the slaughterhouse. And here, you'll create slaughterhouse, "Dum! dum!" and get killed.

~ Srila Prabhupada (Room Conversation -- June 11, 1974, Paris)

alone are the highest UNHCR has seen since 2001. In addition, more than half of the refugees under UNHCR's care (6.3 million) had at end 2013 been in exile for more than five years.

Overall, the biggest refugee populations under UNHCR care and by source country are Afghans, Syrians and Somalis – together

accounting for more than half of the global refugee total. Pakistan, Iran and Lebanon, meanwhile, hosted more refugees than other countries.

In addition to refugees, 2013 saw 1.1 million people submitting applications for asylum, the majority of these in developed countries (Germany became the largest single recipient of new asylum claims). A record 25,300 asylum applications were from children who were separated from or unaccompanied by parents. Syrians lodged 64,300 claims, more than any other nationality, followed by asylum seekers from Democratic Republic of the Congo (60,400) and Myanmar (57,400).

Internal displacement – people forced to flee to other parts of their country – amounted to a record 33.3 million people, accounting for the largest increase of any group in the Global Trends report.

For UNHCR and other humanitarian actors, helping these people represents a special challenge as many are in conflict zones.

Part of UNHCR's work is finding long-term solutions for people who become forcibly displaced. Where possible this is through voluntary return, but other possibilities include local integration or resettlement in third countries. The year 2013 saw the fourth lowest level of refugee returns in almost a quarter century – 414,600 people. Some 98,400 refugees were resettled in 21 countries. Full worldwide data on local integration and returns of internally displaced people (IDP) was not available although 1.4 million of them returned home in countries where UNHCR is operational with IDPs.

The worldwide population of stateless people is not included in the figure of 51.2 million forcibly displaced people (since being stateless doesn't necessarily correlate to being displaced). Statelessness remains hard to quantify with precision, but for 2013, UNHCR's offices worldwide reported a figure of almost 3.5 million stateless people. This is about a third of the number of people estimated to be stateless globally.

The report also says more than half the world's refugees and internally displaced people are children. Many travel alone or in

Murder and consumption of animals happens mainly due to the reason that people believe that animals are meant by God to be utilized by human beings.
However, it is not true. In whatever books it is written that there is no sin to kill animals, in our heartsit is written clearer than in such books, that we need to be sorry for animal the same way as for human being. In fact, we all know it, unless we mute our conscience.

Leo Tolstoy

groups desperately seeking sanctuary only to fall prey to human traffickers.

Source
Stefano Rellandini, Reuters, 13 September 2014
Philip Pullella; Mark Potter, The Daily Mail, 13 September 2014
The Daily Mail, Chris Pleasance, 13 September 2014
News Stories, 20 June 2014
Global forced displacement 1993-2013 (end-year)
Geneva, June 20 (UNHCR)
Copyright © 2014 euronews
Mia De Graaf, The Daily Mail, 20 June 2014

7

Asia's Mad Arms Race

Even As Meat Consumption Grows Exponentially

Economic growth in Asia is witnessing two rapidly rising sectors, arms and meat. Demand for both is growing exponentially. The annual German publication Meat Atlas highlights the environmental impacts of the meat and dairy industries across the globe. It provides "facts and figures about the animals we eat" and is available for free download.

Risk factors explored in the study include over fertilization of farm land, the rise of megafarms, the development of superbugs from widespread antibiotic use, water usage, local shops being replaced by massive supermarket chains, climate change, deforestation, food safety and other health concerns.

While per capita consumption of meat in developed countries dwarfs that of those in poor ones, growing economies in the developing world, especially China and India, mean that global consumption will rise by 150 million tons by the mid 2000s. According to statistics from the Meat Atlas, 80% of the growth in meat production over the next 8 years will be in India and China.

The trend towards more meat in the diets of the developing world essentially mirrors other growth areas of consumption, such as fossil fuels, water and other resources as rapid economic growth results booming middle classes.

It could be argued that the inhabitants of China and India deserve to enjoy what Western Europeans and Americans have enjoyed for years. But some habits should not be emulated. In fact the opposite should be happening and rich countries should be consuming less.

However, the trend towards unregulated markets and unfair trading arrangements being pushed on a global scale is fostering deregulation and a focus on big, quick profits with little concern for the environment, social justice or human health, not to speak of animal welfare.

At present the average inhabitant of the US eats over 165 pounds (75 kg) each year, compared with 132 pounds (60kg) in Germany, 84 pounds (38 kg) in China and under 44 pounds (20 kg) in Africa. Home to 60% of the world's people, Asia already consumes 40% of its chickens, according to the Poultry Site. In terms of individual beings, chicken slaughter absolutely dwarfs other livestock deaths: compare 58 billion chicken deaths per year compared to 320 million cows and buffalo combined.

Exporting Beef, Importing Arms

India has become a world leader in beef export in 2013 with exports crossing 1.8 million tons. It certainly seems surprising at first, that a nation widely known for revering the cow would be a beef exporter at all.

The current industrialized and corporate-led system is doomed to fail. We need a radical overhaul of food and farming if we want to feed a growing world population without destroying the planet.
— *Meat Atlas*

International community is shocked that a nation in which cow slaughter is officially prohibited and is an utter anathema to the majority of the population, will overtake these three icons (Australia, Brazil and US) of cattle ranching and beef eating.

But as the beef exports has skyrocketed, so has the arms imports. Last year India was the world's leading arms purchaser, including a deal that will spend $20 billion dollars on high performance French fighter planes. India is also developing a long-range ballistic missile capable of carrying multiple nuclear warheads, and buying submarines and surface craft. Its military budget is set to rise 17 percent this year to $42 billion.

According to an independent charity, the Naandi Foundation, some 42 percent of India's children are malnourished. Bangladesh, a far poorer country, does considerably better in all these areas.

"It is ridiculous. We are getting into a useless arms race at the expense of fulfilling the needs of poor people," Praful Bidwai of the Coalition of Nuclear Disarmament and Peace told the New York Times.

India aside, the whole of Asia is currently in the middle of an unprecedented arms race that is not only sharpening tensions in the region, but competing with efforts by Asian countries to address poverty and growing economic disparity.

The gap between rich and poor-calculated by the Gini coefficient that measures inequality-has increased from 39 percent to 46 percent in China, India, and Indonesia. While affluent households continue to garner larger and larger portions of the economic pie, "Children born to poor families can be 10 times more likely to die in infancy" than those from wealthy families, according to Changyong Rhee, chief economist of the Asian Development Bank.

This inequality trend is particularly acute in India, where life expectancy is low, infant mortality high, education spotty, and illiteracy widespread, in spite of that country's status as the third largest economy in Asia, behind China and Japan.

China - Leading The Race

China, too, is in the middle of an arms boom that includes beefing up its navy, constructing a new generation of stealth aircraft, and developing a ballistic missile that is potentially capable of neutralizing U.S. carriers near its coast. Beijing's arms budget has grown at a rate of some 12 percent a year and, at $106.41 billion, is now the second largest on the planet. The U.S. budget- not counting the various wars Washington is embroiled in - runs a little over $800 billion, although some have estimated that it is over $1 trillion.

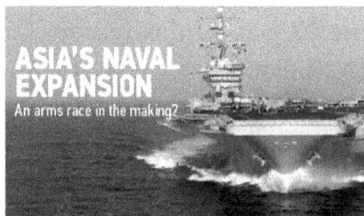

While China has made enormous strides in overcoming poverty, there are some 250 million Chinese officially still considered poor, and the country's formerly red-hot economy is cooling. "Data on April spending and output put another nail into hopes that China's economy is bottoming out," Mark Williams, chief Asia economist at Capital Economics told the Financial Times.

The same is true for most of Asia. For instance, India's annual economic growth rate has fallen from 9 percent to 6.1 percent over the past two and a half years.

Tensions Rise - All Enter The Fray

Tensions between China and other nations in the region have set off a local arms race. Taiwan is buying four U.S.-made Perry-class guided missile frigates, and Japan has shifted much of its military from its northern islands to face southward toward China.

The Philippines are spending almost $1 billion on new aircraft and radar, and recently held joint war games with the U.S. South Korea has just successfully tested a long-range cruise missile. Washington is reviving ties with Indonesia's brutal military because the island nation controls the strategic seaways through which pass most of the region's trade and energy supplies.

Australia is also re-orientating its defense to face China, and Australian Defense Minister Stephen Smith has urged "that India

Disciple: Srila Prabhupada, in a recent study by U.S. agricultural officials, they found that it's uneconomical to eat meat. It takes so much energy and man hours to raise and transport and slaughter the cows that it's very wasteful.

Srila Prabhupada: Wasteful, yes. Therefore I say they have no brain. They are all rascals. Rascal leaders. A little labor in agriculture will be sufficient to produce the family's food stock for the whole year. You work only three months, and you get sufficient food for your whole family. And in the remaining nine months, you chant Hare Krishna.

But these rascals will not do that. They will work hard like asses simply for eating. Nunam pramattah kurute vikarma yad indriya-pritaya aprinoti. They will not accept an easy life.

Disciple: In that agricultural report it said that if people were to eat all the grains they give to the cows and animals, they could get twenty times more calories than by eating meat.

Srila Prabhupada: Yes. Wrong civilization, rascal civilization. And this is due to this rascaldom called nationalism—"This is my land." At any moment a person will be kicked out by death, but still he claims, "It is my land." Janasya moho 'yam aham mameti. This is the illusion. Nothing belongs to him; still he is fighting, "This is mine. This is mine." "I" and "mine"—identifying oneself with the body and wrongly conceiving that "This is mine." This is the basic principle of a wrong civilization. Nothing belongs to us. I have come here to Switzerland. Suppose I remain here for one month and I claim, "Oh, this is mine." What is this?

(cont. on the next page.....)

play the role it could and should as an emerging great power in the security and stability of the region."

But that "role" is by no means clear, and some have read Smith's statement as an attempt to rope New Delhi into a united front against Beijing. The recent test of India's Agni V nuclear-capable ballistic missile is largely seen as directed at China.

India and China fought a brief but nasty border war in 1962, and India claims China is currently occupying some 15,000 square miles in Indian territory. The Chinese, in turn, claim almost 40,000 square miles of the Indian state of Arunachai Pradesh.

India and China also had a short dust up last year when a Chinese warship demanded that the Indian amphibious assault vessel Airavat identify itself shortly after the ship left the port of Hanoi, Vietnam. Nothing came of the incident but Indian President has

(.....cont. from the previous page)

So, similarly, we come to this world as guests. We come to the womb of a mother and live here for seventy years or so. And we claim, "This is my land." But when did it become yours? The land was there long, long before your birth. How has it become yours? But people have no sense. "It is mine—my land, my nation, my family, my society." In this way, they are wasting time.

These things have been introduced by Western civilization. In the Vedic civilization there is no such thing as nationalism. You won't find it there. Have you seen the word "nationalism" in the Bhagavad-gita? No such thing.

Nationalism is the idea of tribes. In Africa there are still groups of tribes. Nationalism is the most crude idea of civilization. It is nothing but developed tribalism. Modern man is not advanced in civilization. This nationalism is another form of tribalism, that's all.

since stressed the need for "maritime security," and "the protection of our coasts, our 'sea lines of communications' and the offshore development areas."

Disciple: Today, so-called civilized people are actually just cannibals because they maintain themselves on eating the cow.

Srila Prabhupada: Yes. And they are suffering. Therefore you'll find that in recent history, every twenty-five years there is a big war with mass slaughter of people. Nature does not tolerate animal slaughter.

Now India has learned to slaughter animals, imitating the Western countries. And now there is war between India and Pakistan. During two wars between Pakistan and Hindustan, millions of people were killed unnecessarily, without any gain.

Disciple: Just recently India exploded an atomic bomb, and now Pakistan is hurrying to get an atomic bomb also.

Srila Prabhupada: Yes.

This is going on.

Disciple: The Indian government promised that nuclear energy would be only for peaceful purposes.

Srila Prabhupada: No, what do they know about peaceful conditions? They are all rascals. They do not know what a peaceful condition is. The actual peaceful condition is described in the Bhagavad-gita:

bhoktaram yajna-tapasam
sarva-loka-maheshvaram
suhridam sarva-bhutanam
jnatva mam shantim ricchati

"A person in full consciousness of Me [Krishna], knowing Me to be the ultimate beneficiary of all sacrifices and austerities, the Supreme Lord of all planets and demigods, and the benefactor and well-wisher of all living entities, attains peace from the pangs of material miseries."

This is peace. Unless there is Krishna consciousness, where is peace? There cannot be peace. All rascaldom. Na mam dushkritino mudhah prapadyante naradhamah. These rascals and fools—mayayapahrita-jnana—have lost all knowledge. How can there be peace? Their endeavors for peace are all useless.

~ Srila Prabhupada (Morning Walk -- June 2, 1974, Geneva)

China's forceful stance in the South China Sea has stirred up tensions with Vietnam, Taiwan, Brunei, and Malaysia as well. A standoff this past April between a Philippine war ship and several Chinese surveillance ships at Scarborough Shoal is still on a low simmer.

China's more assertive posture in the region stems largely from the 1995-96 Taiwan Straits crisis that saw two U.S. carriers humiliate Beijing in its home waters. There was little serious danger of war during the crisis - but the Clinton Administration took the opportunity to demonstrate U.S. naval power. China's naval build-up dates from that incident.

The recent "pivot" by Obama administration toward Asia, including a military buildup on Wake and Guam and the deployment of 2,500 Marines in Australia, has heightened tensions in the region, and Beijing's heavy-handedness in the South China Sea has given Washington an opening to insert itself into the dispute.

Beijing is seriously concerned about who controls the region's seas, in part because some 80 percent of China's energy supplies pass through maritime choke points controlled by the U.S. and its allies.

The tensions in Asia are real, if not as sharp or deep as they have been portrayed in the media. China and India do, indeed, have border "problems," but China also describes New Delhi as "not competitors but partners," and has even offered an alliance to keep "foreign powers"- read the U.S. and NATO - from meddling in the region.

The real question is, can Asia embark on an arms race without increasing the growing gulf between rich and poor and the resulting political instability that is likely to follow in its wake? "Widening

What is the advancement over the dogs? This destruction of another nation by nuclear bombs is the dogs' mentality. Sometimes, even when chained by their respective masters, two dogs will fight as soon as they meet. Have you seen it? It's no better than that.

-Srila Prabhupada (Lecture, Melbourne, Australia)

inequality threatens the sustainability of Asian growth," says Asian Development Bank economist Rhee. "A divided and unequal nation cannot prosper."

More than half a century ago former General and President Dwight Eisenhower noted that "Every gun that is made, every warship that is launched, every rocket fired signifies...a theft from those who are hungry and are not fed, those who are cold and are not clothed...this is not a way of life at all...it is humanity hanging from an iron cross."

Americans have ignored Eisenhower's warning. Asian nations would do well to pay attention.

Source

Conn Hallinan, Dispatches from the Edge. May 24 2012

Times of India report dated April 1, 2013,

Smith, Theresa Clair (1980). "Arms Race Instability and War". Journal of Conflict Resolution

8

Meat

An Orgy of Violence And Murder

An Ornithologist's Observation

Watching and listening to birds is a pleasant experience. In our civilization, human settlements have pushed the remaining wildlife to pockets of 'forests'. Waking up early in the morning I enjoy observing the nature that survives on the fringes of civilization. I live in a housing project a densely populated suburban community outside of Pittsburgh PA.

I am convinced that a meat based diet (i.e, beef, pork, chicken, fish and other animals) is a regression in evolution of human consciousness and a move towards the primitive state of violence and barbarism. Civilization learnt to grow food and evolved away from hunting into a secure diet of grain and vegetables where meat eating was only ceremonial.

A Bird Watching Experiment, 16th May 2004

It was Sunday, 6:00AM. The weather was cool, 60 degrees and mostly cloudy. There were starlings, sparrows, blue jays, robins and squirrels in and around my house.

While sipping my morning coffee I noticed my mother had gone shopping. I decided to take a few packages of opened snack crackers and scatter them in the lawn for birds. I appreciate the chirping of the birds and watching them feed is also an interesting pastime.

These creatures are intelligent and resourceful unlike many of us who live in a disposable culture where little is reused and utilized. I have observed birds use ground litter to construct their nests. Also birds often build their nests in gutters or below a overhanging roof surface to further shelter from the elements.

I spread the crackers (Town House) on the lawn below a second story window to watch the birds in silence. Sitting by the window, I saw that the house sparrows were the first to arrive on the scene in about 5 minutes. Next followed by starlings. All birds snacked together, some grabbed a piece from the lawn (it was a 15 yard long line of cracker pieces), flew away and came back for more.

Some birds would retrieve a piece and deposit the cracker on the concrete to eat but some others would swiftly try to steal those peices for themselves.

For some reason, I always see lots of starlings when the weather is cloudy and very few when it's sunny and clear. Last time I saw some starlings someone had left a styrofoam carton of several chicken wings near the sidewalk from the local convenience store (people often litter in the housing project) and a small flock of starlings were eating the chicken wings like the crows.

The starlings have sharp yellow beaks and a rainbow oilish glow to their dark feathers which might be a natural secretion to waterproof them from the rain like a duck. Well when the starlings appeared on the scene, I remembered that sidewalk incident and thought of feeding them some luncheon meat from the refrigerator. I saw some ham in the fridge and picked it up.

Pork has got a bad reputation with the Jewish and Islamic people. They strictly avoid it. I remember reading an edition of Expedition magazine, published by the university of Pennsylvania archaeology team which tells how Spanish Conquistadors abolished native

Central American cannibalistic practices and some of the Aztecs told them how pork from the newly imported pig reminded them of the taste of human flesh.

I took the pieces of luncheon pork (very greasy to touch) and strewn them along the sidewalk parallel to the 15 yard area of cracker pieces in the lawn. I went back to my window and to my coffee cup.

The Starlings almost immediately came to inspect this new food source. Different individuals inspected this suspiciously and no one came to forward to try it for a good ten minutes. But it all changed when a larger starling picked it up, all others entered the fray. They were in a flock of about 10 to 15. Some starlings were sitting on the power lines above and they too swooped down to pick up some pork.

Now the house sparrows were uninterested in the pork and continued to pick at the crackers happily, without caring for the starlings.

Around this time a pair of robins landed on the scene and scared away some of the starlings and sparrows. The robins did not seem interested in any crackers or pork but just wanted to put up a territorial display. The robins were earlier feasting on worms in the dew covered grass.

After the robins flew away, the feeding resumed with the same efficiency as before. The next appearance was that of a solitary blue jay who scattered the whole gang of starlings and sparrows to get some snack crackers. The last outside species to appear that morning was the neighborhood squirrel. She trotted up to the edge of the yard to look around but was probably full from the shelled peanuts left under the pin oak and just wanted to put in a appearance.

After the Starlings had eaten all the pork from the sidewalk the sparrows were still pecking at the remains of the snack crackers on the sides. An hour has passed since the feast began. The starlings having tasted flesh seemed no longer interested in crackers but still stayed on the scene. They appeared to be looking around aggressively.

Suddenly, a large adult Starling began to take charge violently. Twice the size of a sparrow and with a long needle like beak the Starling tried to kill a sparrow for food. The first time it was unsuccessful in pinning the sparrow down and the second time it used enough force to draw blood and screeching sound of pain from the wounded sparrow. Then the other starlings began to join in with screeching calls of their own maybe to join in the hunt. The starlings unlike the sparrows are easily startled by humans. I lifted the screen of my window and gave the sparrow a chance to escape followed by the large starling in hot pursuit.

I received a mandate from a major conglomerate and visited their various operations, one of which turned out to be a slaughterhouse. It was the most shocking, terrifying and violent experience of my life. It was tangible proof of the abject failure of human beings to develop empathy for the suffering of other living beings. I think I now understand what Hannah Arendt meant in her work "Eichmann in Jerusalem" where she coined the term "the banality of evil".

The sheer horror that morning affected me profoundly. I began seeing every mundane piece of daily life's experience through the prism of animal cruelty. Passing a crowded restaurant, and knowing that it concealed a smorgasbord of murderous opportunities. Seeing an attractive woman at the ballet and being repulsed by the sight of her fur coat. Knowing that every butcher shop was a retailer of body parts from murder victims; every fast food chain, in my mind, became a gastronomic tobacconist and every bit as lethal.

So, I guess my client's slaughterhouse made me a vegetarian on the spot. It did not occur to me that dairy was an equally vile gulag for animals. Once I saw the carnage of veal, artificial insemination of cows; the removal of bobby calves from their mothers, the cruelty of induction and the violence of killing "unviable" calves, dairy was another atrocity on the list.

~ Philip Wollen, former vice-president of Citibank

It was a scary experience for me, from a peaceful feast of snack crackers to a violent orgy of meat inspired murder. That day it dawned on me that it is possible to manipulate the thoughts and behaviour of the masses by taking control of their diet. Wars and acts of aggression can be promoted by promoting a meat based diet.

But why would any body want war? War means death and destruction but to some it smells like money. The world today has permanent war economies and if the war stops, the world economy collapses. The multinational corporations control the arms trade and they control our food. That is why we see so many TV advertisements for meat products whereas fruits and vegetables are never advertised.

Today's world is getting ground under the corporate jackboot. These huge corporations make obscene profits out of human misery and they want the world to remain in misery. They run our health care industry. They run our oil and gas companies. They run our bloated weapons industry. They run Wall Street and the major investment firms. They run our manufacturing firms. They also, ominously, run our government.

World is simply not a safe place in the shadows of these greedy monsters. They want profits - when economy thrives and they want profits - when economy dies. Profits in a dying economy means war. That's the only way to go about it

By Richard J. Barnet, Pittsburgh PA,

Meat-eaters. Walking around like their lifestyle isn't causing any harm. Like it's normal and natural to be consuming violence and death. How would you feel if the day you were born somebody else had already planned the day of your execution? That's what it's like to be a cow, pig, chicken or turkey on this planet. I think this type of behavior is inexcusable and unbecoming of a species that claims to understand right from wrong. The animals have not done one single thing to us to deserve the wrath and cruelty that we hurl on them."

~ Gary Yourofsky

9

School Field Trip Tour of Slaughterhouse

Traumatizes Children

In Omaha, Nebraska: Eighteen grade 5 students of Mavis Beacon Elementary School are undergoing counseling after a school field trip visit to a beef slaughterhouse. The children reportedly were horrified to see how cows were processed into beef. Some of the students vomited, and most cried.

Their teacher, Maxwell Barnes, faces disciplinary action for organizing the school field trip. "I didn't see anything wrong with it." Barnes stated. "Earlier this year we had a field trip to a chocolate factory. Kids have a curiosity about where their food comes from. I don't think there should be anything wrong with showing them where meat comes from."

The children were escorted through the facility from the loading bay, where cattle enter the building, through to the stunning process where the animals receive a pneumatic bolt to the brain, rendering them brain dead. "Some of the kids started crying then," said slaughterhouse foreman Dan Smith. "We told them it was all a natural part of how beef is made and ends up in yummy hamburgers, but that didn't seem to help much."

The field trip then went awry after the brain dead animals were chained up by their back legs and then cut into to be bled to death. "I saw one little boy throw up." Smith said. "And then after that there was screaming and running and all these other kids throwing up all over the place. We tried to calm them down but it was out of

"A cruel and wretched person who maintains his existence at the cost of others' lives deserves to be killed for his own well-being, otherwise he will go down by his own actions.

According to Manu, the great author of civic codes and religious principles, even the killer of an animal is to be considered a murderer because animal food is never meant for the civilized man, whose prime duty is to prepare himself for going back to Godhead. He says that in the act of killing an animal, there is a regular conspiracy by the party of sinners, and all of them are liable to be punished as murderers exactly like a party of conspirators who kill a human being combinedly. He who gives permission, he who kills the animal, he who sells the slaughtered animal, he who cooks the animal, he who administers distribution of the foodstuff, and at last he who eats such cooked animal food are all murderers, and all of them are liable to be punished by the laws of nature. No one can create a living being despite all advancement of material science, and therefore no one has the right to kill a living being by one's independent whims. For the animal-eaters, the scriptures have sanctioned restricted animal sacrifices only, and such sanctions are there just to restrict the opening of slaughterhouses and not to encourage animal-killing. The procedure under which animal sacrifice is allowed in the scriptures is good both for the animal sacrificed and the animal-eaters. It is good for the animal in the sense that the sacrificed animal is at once promoted to the human form of life after being sacrificed at the altar, and the animal-eater is saved from grosser types of sins (eating meats supplied by organized slaughterhouses which are ghastly places for breeding all kinds of material afflictions to society, country and the people in general). The material world is itself a place always full of anxieties, and by encouraging animal slaughter the whole atmosphere becomes polluted more and more by war, pestilence, famine and many other unwanted calamities."

~ Srila Prabhupada (Srimad Bhagavatam 1:7:37 Text and Purport)

control by then. These kids were just freaked out, they didn't even finish the tour.

Imagine if these kids were taken to a fruit orchard or a vegetable garden, it would have been a memorable trip!

Source
Newsweek, 16 April 2009

10

Meat-eating and War

A Buddhist Perspective

During thousands and hundreds of years,
    The hatreds and viciousness in meats
In people's dining utensils,
Are as deep as sea,
And are hardly to cease.
If one wants to know why there are wars in the world,
Just listen to the thrilling screams
From a slaughter house

This is a Buddhist poem, which reveals the connection between Meat-eating and War.

Meat-eating causes hatred, ill feeling and thoughts of vengeance, and these negative thoughts lead to war.

The hatred and vengeance arises when an animal is slaughtered. The helpless animal, suffering intensely, is filled with thoughts of fear, hatred and vengeance. When people partake of meat so produced, their consciousness also gets saturated with these negative qualities.

Over a period of time, these damaging emotions of hatred, fear and vengeance accumulate in the psyche of the meat-eaters, making them more and more depressed, hateful of others, very irritable and angry. And when a large number of people (e.g. people in a nation) are dominated by these emotions, that starts a war.

In such a war, these meat-eaters butcher each other exactly in the manner of the animals.

A Meat-eater ingests all kinds of negative vibrations and these vibrations block his heart and close it, make it as hard as stone and become a great obstruction in enlightenment.

A philosopher with evil inclinations, who preaches the doctrines that support violence, massacre, and anti-religious behaviors, may emerge under such circumstances.

If one renounces meat-eating, these pollutants will not continue to accumulate in his body and heart, but these pollutants will not be cleansed automatically. One has to practice some Dharmas (e.g. mantras, repentances etc) which can cleanse these negative karmas.

There are many prayers and chants which are very powerful and efficient for cleansing the bad karma. These Dharma-streams

Slaughtering poor animals is also due to the mode of ignorance. The animal killers do not know that in the future the animal will have a body suitable to kill them. That is the law of nature. In human society, if one kills a man he has to be hanged. That is the law of the state. Because of ignorance, people do not perceive that there is a complete state controlled by the Supreme Lord. Every living creature is a son of the Supreme Lord, and He does not tolerate even an ant's being killed. One has to pay for it. So, indulgence in animal killing for the taste of the tongue is the grossest kind of ignorance. A human being has no need to kill animals because God has supplied so many nice things. If one indulges in meat-eating anyway, it is to be understood that he is acting in ignorance and is making his future very dark. Of all kinds of animal killing, the killing of cows is most vicious because the cow gives us all kinds of pleasure by supplying milk.

~ Srila Prabhupada (Bhagavad gita 14.16)

can wash your heart, soften your heart, make your heart open for enlightenment, and make you a completely virtuous person.

Lord Buddha - An Incarnation Who Preached Against The Slaughterhouse Culture

Lord Buddha, a powerful incarnation of the Personality of Godhead, appeared in the province of Gaya (Bihar) and he preached his own conception of nonviolence and deprecated even the animal sacrifices sanctioned in the Vedas. At the time when Lord Buddha appeared, the people in general were atheistic and preferred animal flesh to anything else. On the plea of Vedic sacrifice, every place was practically turned into a slaughterhouse, and animal-killing was indulged in unrestrictedly. Lord Buddha preached nonviolence, taking pity on the poor animals. He preached that he did not believe in the tenets of the Vedas and stressed the adverse psychological effects incurred by animal-killing. Less intelligent men of the age of Kali, who had no faith in God, followed his principle, and for the time being they were trained in moral discipline and nonviolence, the preliminary steps for proceeding further on the path of God realization.

Killing of animals before the advent of Lord Buddha was the most prominent feature of the society. People claimed that these were Vedic sacrifices. When the Vedas are not accepted through the authoritative disciplic succession, the casual readers of the Vedas are misled by the flowery language of that system of knowledge.

To such bewildered persons of atheistic propensity, Lord Buddha is the emblem of theism. He therefore first of all wanted to check the habit of animal-killing. The animal-killers are dangerous elements on the path going back to Godhead. There are two types of animal-killers. The soul is also sometimes called the "animal" or the living being. Therefore, both the slaughterer of animals and those who have lost their identity of soul are animal-killers.

Maharaja Pariksit said that only the animal-killer cannot relish the transcendental message of the Supreme Lord. Therefore if people are to be educated to the path of Godhead, they must be taught first and foremost to stop the process of animal-killing as above mentioned. It is nonsensical to say that animal-killing has nothing to do with spiritual realization. By this dangerous theory many so-called sannyasis have sprung up by the grace of Kali-yuga who preach animal-killing under the garb of the Vedas. The subject matter has already been discussed in the conversation between Lord Caitanya and Maulana Chand Kazi Shaheb. The animal sacrifice as stated in the Vedas is different from the unrestricted animal-killing in the slaughterhouse. Because the asuras or the so-called scholars of Vedic literatures put forward the evidence of animal-killing in the Vedas, Lord Buddha superficially denied the authority of the Vedas. This rejection of the Vedas by Lord Buddha was adopted in order to save people from the vice of animal-killing as well as to save the poor animals from the slaughtering process of their big brothers who clamor for universal brotherhood, peace, justice and equity. There is no justice when there is animal-killing. Lord Buddha wanted to stop it completely, and therefore his cult of ahimsa was propagated not only in India but also outside the country.

We are glad that people are taking interest in the nonviolent movement of Lord Buddha. But will they take the matter very seriously and close the animal slaughterhouses altogether? If not, there is no meaning to the ahimsa cult.

Source:
A.C.Bhaktivedanta Swami Prabhupada, Srimad-Bhagavatam 1:3:24 Purport
HH Aung-Thwin, Buddhism And World Peace, 2001.
Thanissaro Bhikkhu (1997)

11

Vegetarian Diet

Impacts California Prison

I n the late 90's, amid rising crime rates and finite lockup space, the private prison industry was looking like a pretty lucrative business opportunity for anyone who could take advantage. Having received a dire report from Georgia-based prison design firm Rosser International Inc., San Bernardino County (California) was expecting a shortfall in inmate beds and a doubling of their inmate population by the year 2020. Against this background, the County began accepting bids for a 500-inmate private prison.

Terry Mooreland, CEO of Maranatha Private Corrections LLC was among the individuals who bid on the project. There was only one catch. Mooreland's bid included a stipulation that if he was

I was an inmate at adelanto in 1999. I have been clean and sober since the day I walked out of there in July 1999 . Julianne Aranda was working and teaching us nutrition, I have been clean and sober since I left over 13 years ago and am now a drug and alcohol counsellor.
~ Eric Vandennoort, October 11, 2012

awarded the bid, inmates serving sentences at his facility would be offered a vegetrian diet.

As fate would have it, Mooreland won the bid and in 1997 began to build what became the Victor Valley Medium Community Correctional Facility in Adelanto, California; which is about 120 miles northeast of Los Angeles. Once operational, this facility saw remarkable results for seven years, before a dispute over inmate phone revenue led the State of California to cancel their contract

with Mooreland.

It is unbelievable that something as silly as phone revenue could cause a State to end one of the most remarkable prison success programs in the country, where inmates got out and stayed out. At the time, the State of California had a recidivism rate of 95%. This is the percentage of former prisoners who are rearrested. The Victor Valley facility enjoyed a recidivism rate of less than 2%.

Key Factor Behind This Success

So, what was the key factor behind this success? A vegetarian diet.

I was at this prison in 2000, it was a great program and unfortunately politics was trying to shut it down at the time. I guess they succeeded. I would recommend this sort of program all over the country
~ Steve, April 11, 2013

Upon arrival, new inmates attended an orientation where they received two clear choices. They could live on one side of the prison which operated using the standard California Department of Corrections (CDC) guidelines and food menus; or, they could live on the side of the prison operated under the "NEWSTART" program which included a vegan diet, bible studies, job training and anger management.

In a video-taped interview obtained by Vegetarian Spotlight, Victor Valley nutrition services coordinator Julianne Aranda explains that "what we eat not only affects us physically, but it affects our mental attitude, our aggressiveness and our ability to make good decisions".

In interview after interview it was clear that the NEWSTART program staff was in agreement that the mind and body must be cleaned up in order for the inmates to achieve positive behavioral changes.

Initially, although the State of California was very supportive of the NEWSTART concept, they told Moorland they didn't believe that even five inmates (of the 500) would accept that kind of a diet. In fact, they told Moorland that inmates would probably "burn the place down before they became vegetarians".

However, once the program was in progress, the opposite became true. On average, 85% of the inmates chose the NEWSTART side while only 15% chose the CDC program.

The remarkable behavioral changes could even be seen outside in the prison yard where according to prison officials, nobody "owned"

Correctional Facilities? A program that addressed the mind, body, and soul of a man which led to true change and a new life- and it gets cancelled for money? Why are there no groups or politicians making this a priority and getting this program back. USA, we jail more of our citizens than any other country. 1 in 100 of us are affected. Its reprehensible to think we allow Americans to suffer the degradation for some money making agenda. Ethics, character; nope just the money.

~ Robbin, a former inmate

or controlled the yard. Typical lines drawn between blacks, whites, hispanics, gang members and other groups were non existent.

On the NEWSTART side, everyone played basketball together and had great fellowship. The CDC side of the house had the same racial divisions experienced at any other prison.

In testimonials, inmates assert that the surprisingly good-tasting food led them to feel better, have greater energy, increased stamina and reduced problems with acne. Indeed the effectiveness of a vegetarian diet in rehabilitation has been scientifically validated.

Although the State of California apparently preferred to pursue phone revenue over rehabilitated inmates, the success of the Victor Valley facility gives us something to think about. Could this kind of a diet make the world a more peaceful and a more strife-free place to live.

Source:

Vegetarian Spotlight January 9, 2011

Bonnie L Beezhold , Vegetarian diets are associated with healthy mood states: a cross-sectional study in Seventh Day Adventist adults, June 1, 2010,

12

Arizona Jail

Goes Meat-Free

Think vegetarian eating is expensive? Maricopa County, Arizona Sheriff Joe Arpaio would disagree. In fact, Sheriff Joe recently announced that all jails in Maricopa County will now serve 100 percent meat-free meals, and he expects this menu change to save taxpayers $100,000.

"Little by little this is the first step to going vegetarian. There will be no more meat on the menu," Sheriff Joe told Fox 10 in Phoenix.

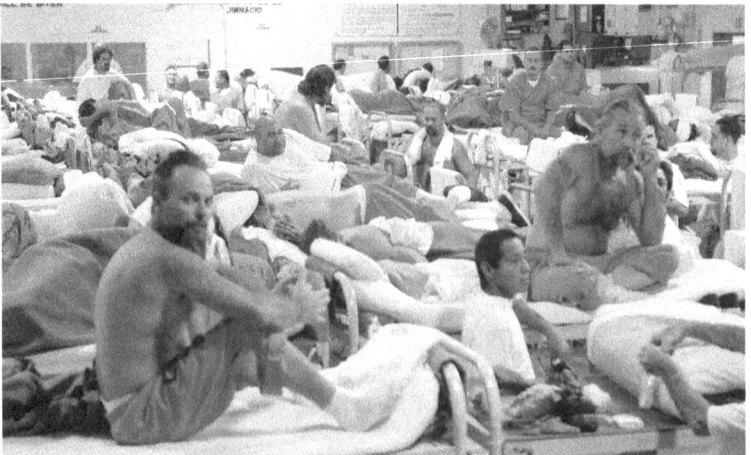

He expects the full transition from meat to protein-packed soy-based meals to take a few months.

While Sheriff Joe is clear about the fact that this change is strictly a cost-saving measure, he has publicly spoken out against the cruel, intensive confinement of farmed animals. In 2006, he lent his support to a successful Arizona ballot initiative measure, Proposition 204, which, as of this year, effectively bans the use of veal and gestation crates throughout the state.

Another advantage to eliminating meat from jail menus? The inmates might start seeing some positive health benefits! According to the American Dietetic Association, vegetarians tend to have a lower body mass index, lower overall cancer rates, lower blood pressure, and a lower risk of death from ischemic heart disease.

Source

Katie Vann, Compassion Over Killing, September 26, 2013

Guest: Jesus Christ..., it is said that he made the miracle of the fish and ate. So why is it that one should not eat meat?

Prabhupada: Jesus Christ said, "You shall not kill." Why you are killing?

Guest : But then why did he eat fish?

Prabhupada: He can eat the whole world, but you cannot do that. You must follow his instruction, "Thou shall not kill."

Might have done so. One thing is Christ is powerful. Under certain circumstances, even if he had eaten some fish, that is not fault for him. Tejiyasam na dosaya [SB 10.33.29]. In the sastra it says, those who are very powerful, if they sometimes do something which is prohibited for common man, that is special case. On the plea that "Lord Christ sometimes took some fish somewhere; therefore we will have to maintain a big slaughterhouse," this is not very good logic.

... And he taught in the desert. Suppose there was no food and he had to eat some fish. But does it mean on that strength throughout the whole world the Christians will maintain big, big, up-to-date machinery for slaughterhouse?

—Srila Prabhupada (Lecture, Srimad-Bhagavatam 1.16.20 -- Los Angeles, July 10, 1974)

13

Meatless Monday

Anger Management

Anger is a natural human response to crisis. It gives you a shot of adrenaline and cortisol, your fight or flight hormone. You're focused, three espressos worth of revved. If you were graded by the Department of Homeland Security, you'd be in a state of red alert.

This is useful in a crunch situation, but a steady diet of anger isn't good for you. It locks up your muscles and sends your blood pressure and heart rate skyward. Too much cortisol over too much time results in a fat gut and a slow brain. Anger can make you fat, stupid or dead. So chill, guys. One way to do that is to give up meat.

Recent research by Arizona State University showed omnivores who went meatless felt better emotionally. Of the 39 people studied, one group kept to their omnivorous ways, a second group ate fish but no other source of animal protein, the third group ate no fish, no meat, no eggs.

Now We Get Mondays Off!

The first two groups reported no change in emotion or cognition. The plant-based party reported they felt more relaxed and focused than they did eating meat.

The Harvard School of Public Health examined 1,300 men in their 60s over the course of seven years and found the angriest guys were likelier to develop heart disease than those who could ride life's highs and lows without losing it.

> *How can he practice true compassion*
> *who eats the flesh of an animal to fatten his own flesh?*
> *Riches cannot be found in the hands of the thriftless,*
> *nor can compassion be found in the hearts of those who eat meat.*
> *He who feasts on a creature's flesh is like he who wields a weapon.*
> *Goodness is never one with the minds of these two.*
> *If you ask, "What is kindness and what is unkindness?"*
> *It is not-killing and killing. Thus, eating flesh is never virtuous.*
> *Life is perpetuated by not eating meat.*
> *The jaws of Hell close on those who do.*
> *If the world did not purchase and consume meat,*
> *no one would slaughter and offer meat for sale.*
> *When a man realizes that meat is the butchered flesh*
> *of another creature, he will abstain from eating it.*
> *Insightful souls who have abandoned the passion to hurt others*
> *will not feed on flesh that life has abandoned.*
> *Greater than a thousand ghee offerings consumed in sacrificial*
> *fires is to not sacrifice and consume any living creature.*
> *All life will press palms together in prayerful adoration*
> *of those who refuse to slaughter or savor meat.*
> *~ Verses from Tirukural, (An ancient Tamil classic by Sage Tiruvalluvar)*

In another study, the Harvard School of Public Health showed eating bacon, salami, sausage, hot dogs, any meat that's been processed or cured or salted, jacks up your risk of heart disease by 42 percent and your risk of diabetes by 19 percent. Feeling anger poses a lot of the same health risks as eating meat does.

Centuries before modern science noted what meat does to your body and mood, another science, Ayurveda, Sanskrit for the science of life, noted what it does to your karma, Sanskrit for action. Karma says we will experience the consequences of our actions, what goes around comes around.

Ayurveda, or balance, separates food and states of being into three categories. There's sattvic - lightness and balance (spirit) rajasic - change and energy (life), and tamasic -- heavy and dark (death). Guess which category meat falls under? The Surangama Sutra tells us that "if we eat the flesh of living creatures, we are destroying the seeds of compassion." That's the opposite of sattva, which strives for ahimsa, universal love, non-violence.

There's no meat in a sattvic diet, just fresh organic fruits and vegetables, beans, whole grains, raw nuts and seeds and organic dairy. These foods are believed to energize and nourish the body without taxing it, providing the gateway to higher consciousness.

Does this piss you off? It could be you have a meat-related anger management issue and everyone around you is too afraid to tell you. Perhaps you'd benefit by swapping that steak for something sattvic.

Giving up meat doesn't mean depriving yourself of pleasure. You can be enlightened and peaceful and still eat fabulous food. You'll

This killing of animals is for the non-civilized society. They cannot... They do not know how to grow food. They were killing animals. When man is advanced in his knowledge and education, why they should kill? Especially in America, we see so many nice foodstuffs. Fruits, grains, milk. And from milk, you can get hundreds of nice preparations, all nutritious.
-Prabhupada (Room Conversation, July 5, 1975, Chicago)

be on your way to a healthier body, a happier life and a lighter karma, too.

Source
Ellen Kanner, Author and syndicated columnist, the Edgy Veggie May 31, 2010
Ellen Kanner, "Meat People Push Back" April 15, 2010

14

The Link

Between Diet and Crime

Could violence and crime be caused in some measure by nutritional deficiencies in general? And furthermore, could either producing or consuming meat incline a person to violence and crime?

Before we jump into some of the research, let's take a step back and consider the issue. As we all know, our behavior is mostly controlled by our brain, an organ weighing only about three pounds. Now we know that every organ in the human body requires nutrition to function properly and when it doesn't get it, it functions abnormally. So is there any reason that the brain should be an exception to this? The human brain is perhaps the most

"Men!"

remarkable and the most complex material in the universe. Isn't it just possible that if it doesn't get the right nutrition, it might not work as well as it should?

Several researchers had the hunch that it wouldn't take much in the way of nutritional deficiencies to cause changes in behavior including criminal behavior, so they investigated the matter.

Oxford University researcher Bernard Gesch, publishing his research in The British Journal of Psychiatry, showed that nutritional supplements alone would reduce antisocial behavior in prison, including violence and other offenses, by 35%. They were able to prove that this wasn't due to a placebo effect because those receiving phony supplements showed no improvement at all. Something real was happening.

In another study conducted by the Dutch Ministry of Justice in Holland, those prisoners receiving nutritional supplements showed a 34% reduction in violent behavior.

Other researchers have seen results with supplements as well. For instance, one study showed that nutritional supplements were more powerful in reducing repeat offenses by criminals on probation than counseling.

Although no one is suggesting that poor diet alone can account for complex social problems, chief inspector of British prisons Lord Ramsbotham says that he is now "absolutely convinced that there is a direct link between diet and antisocial behavior, both that bad diet causes bad behavior and that good diet prevents it."

And it wasn't just on the other side of the Atlantic where researchers were coming up with links between diet and crime. Professor of Criminology and Sociology at California State University, Stephen Shoenthaler, has been studying the effects of vitamins on inmates in California for the last 20 years. In a study among young offenders in California, Shoenthaler found that young adult men receiving vitamin supplements showed a 38% drop in serious behavior problems.

And in a large study of prison diets in California, New York, Oklahoma, Virginia, and Florida, Shoenthaler found that prisoner's eating habits could be used to predict future violent behavior. Now normally, past violent behavior is considered the best prediction of future violence. But professor Shoenthaler found that a poor diet is an even better predictor of violent behavior.

A Vegetarian Diet Fits The Bill

So where do vegetarian diets fit into all of this? Well, since vegetarian diets represent nutrition par excellence, we would expect some pretty definite effects.

Meet Robert King. King was sentenced to a 28 year term at Powhatan Correctional Center in Virginia for burglary. When he got to prison King weighed 275 pounds and was addicted to cocaine. Since that time he has eaten his way back to physical and mental health. King became a near vegan through a special program at the prison, and it had a big effect on him. He lost 50 pounds, freed himself of drug dependency and earned 53 credits at J. Sargeant Reynolds Community College with an A average. King credited his new diet for his big turnaround and said "it all begins and ends with my diet." The Corrections Facility Director Tom Parlett confirmed the effect of the better diet on the inmates in the program, and said that he had seen their whole attitudes change.

So prisoners who give up eating meat improve their behavior. How about the effect of meat on those who produce it, slaughterhouse workers for instance? Would merely producing meat incline a person to violence and crime?

The part of the American economy that's still booming.

University of Windsor Criminology professor Amy Fitzgerald says statistics show that there may be a link between slaughterhouses and brutal crime . In a recent study, Fitzgerald crunched numbers from the FBI's Uniform Crime Report database, census data, and arrest and offence reports from 581 U.S. counties from 1994 to 2002. According to the professor, as the number of slaughterhouse workers in a community increases, the crime rate also increases. Fitzgerald controlled for factors such as the influx of new residents and other factors when slaughterhouses first open but the data was clear.

Nor could the violence be blamed on factory work itself. Fitzgerald compared slaughterhouse communities to those with comparable industries — dangerous, repetitive work that didn't involve killing animals. These were not associated with a rise in crime at all. The numbers leave few explanations other than the slaughterhouses being somehow involved.

According to Professor Fitzgerald, "The unique thing about slaughterhouses is that the workers are not dealing with inanimate objects, but instead dealing with live animals coming in and then killing them and processing what's left of them."

For now, this is all we know about the link between diet and crime. Much more research needs to be done before we can fully understand the matter.

In the meantime, please take note. We don't condone any crime by anyone for any reason, and we believe that regardless of their diet, all people must be held responsible for their crimes. However, if these and other studies linking diet and crime are confirmed, a great breakthrough may be at hand. Crime takes a massive toll on society, in both money and human suffering, for criminal and victim alike.

We don't claim that malnutrition is the 'only' cause of crime, nor is it the 'only' solution. But if better nutrition in general, and a vegetarian diet in particular, can bring about a substantial reduction in violent crime, that would be something to cheer about. For isn't a good diet, made up of good food, a better and a less expensive solution than just hiring more police and building more prisons?

Source:
Vegetarians Of Washington, July 24, 2011
Children with a high IQ are more likely to become vegetarian University of Southampton. Soton.ac.uk (December 15, 2006).

15

Karma

What Goes Around Comes Around

The basic principle of karma is that we get back exactly what we put out. If we put out love, we get back love. If we put out violence, we get back violence. Try it out - at least the first part. Be nice to everyone you meet one day and see what happens. But if you did go around another day punching people in the face, I guarantee you'd come home with two black eyes.

One of the major causes of bad karma is unnecessary violence to animals. Throughout history no man with a full stomach (or who lived near a grocery store) ever went hunting. And throughout history animals were never slaughtered en masse in slaughter-houses. It is only modern man who has become expert at the massive killing of animals for sport and for satisfying his tongue.

We are so removed from the killing of animals that when we eat a turkey leg we may not even be conscious that this was once the LEG OF A TURKEY WE ARE EATING. Most people don't think of how the animal once ran around on the very leg that they are eating; that the animal might have been someone's mother, son, daughter or father. If we saw it that way we probably wouldn't want to eat it (oh did I spoil your appetite!).

Some of us love our pets and kill other animals for sport. Some of us give money to save endangered species and eat cows, sheep, chickens and turkeys. Some eat hot dogs and have a pet pig. Something's wrong with this picture.

If you saw a turkey on the road, wouldn't you try to avoid running it over? I sure would. And wouldn't you feel bad if you ran it over? I bet there would be a lot more vegetarians out there if we all had to personally kill what ate. So in a sense meat eating really runs contrary to our natural instincts, particularly when there is enough vegetarian food to eat.

Since Violence That Goes Out Must Come Back, There Is A Connection Between The Way We Treat Animals And War

George Bernard Shaw wrote:
We pray on Sundays that we may have light
To guide our footsteps on the path we tread.
We are sick of war, we don't want to fight,
And yet we gorge ourselves upon the dead.

Karma

Like carrion crows we live and feed on meat,
Regardless of the suffering and pain
We cause by doing so. In this way we treat
Defenseless animals for sport or gain.
How can we hope in this world to attain
The peace we say we are anxious for?
We pray for it on the catacombs of the slain
While outraging the moral law.
Thus cruelty begets its offspring—war!

The way karma works is that we don't have to personally kill the animal to take part in the violence and get the reaction. If we have anything to do with the violence (working in the meat industry, transporting animals or meat, cooking or serving meat, buying meat or eating meat), there is a reaction we'll suffer; and a reaction the world suffers.

If I got into the details of the reactions you'd really lose your appetite this time (one reaction that is obvious is that meat eaters suffer higher rates of deadly diseases like cancer, stroke and heart attacks than vegetarians). The fact is that you do yourself, the animals and the world a great favor by being vegetarian.

My spiritual master said that if people stopped eating meat, there would be no more war. I realize that this is hard to swallow. We can't make an experiment to prove this because we can't control animal slaughter. But we can make another experiment that shows something important that gives more credence to this theory.

We can make a controlled experiment on ourselves. I want to ask you if you would try doing the following experiment on yourself. It could change you life.

Stop Eathing All Meat, Fish, And Eggs, For At Least A Week And Notice How It Affects You.

Actually, I have done some casual research in this area. I have asked many people to refrain from meat eating for a week just to test it out and see how they feel. Many were doubters thinking it would have no effect on the way they thought or the way they saw the world. Many didn't even believe they could live without meat - or even be healthy without it. But given enough time with them to discuss the pros of being vegetarian and the cons of meat eating, I could convince almost any open minded person to try it for at least a week or two (move in with your vegetarian friends, buy a cook book, eat at vegetarian restaurants, whatever it takes! It'll be worth it).

So What Happened?

Aside from telling me they felt better, the vast majority said they became sensitive to the fact that they were causing pain to animals by eating them. This is amazing. Just by not eating meat for a week or two, people who had eaten meat all their lives without a second thought - who never associated the food they were eating to a live animal who gave their life and suffered - were somehow now looking at meat eating it an entirely different light.

They Also Told Me They Felt More Peaceful

It's difficult to be objective about something when you are doing it yourself. So when you stop eating meat for a while, you start looking at the issue from a different perspective. But they also felt different because they were no longer taking part in the violence of animal slaughter.

This Is The Real Reason They Felt So Different

According to ancient India texts on consciousness and health, the eating of meat dulls the part of the brain that makes us sensitive to the suffering of animals. I haven't done any serious research on this. All I can say is that I haven't met any vegetarian hunters in my life - and I have been around the block quite a few times. Come to think of it, I haven't met any vegetarian butchers either.

Of course, my personal experience can't conclusively prove that vegetarians are less violent people, or that there is a connection between war and vegetarianism? But may be this experiment could. We'll make Osama and his buddies vegetarians and see what happens. I bet they'd become peaceniks. Hey, this could be the best counter terrorism plan out there!

And the animals would love it too.

By Mahatma Das, (Member, International Society For Krishna Consciousness)

Killology - The Science of Creating Killers

Human Reluctance To Take A Life Can Be Reversed Through Training

During the Iraq War a number of articles appeared in the German news magazine, Der Spiegel and Stern, about "killology". This is the application of psychological techniques by the American military to overcoming soldiers inhibitions on killing. One of these articles, in the magazine Stern, related how new recruits are given a white rabbit to pet, to carry and to get to know, and then, at the end of the week, they have to kill it and eat it.

This is part of a wider training programme on killing.

The article was written earlier than the Iraq war but explores the theme of the psychological connection between killing animals and killing people.

Source

Brian Davey, September 2001, Slaughtering Animals and Slaughtering People Killology Reseearch Group, Mascoutah, IL.

Spanish Butcher - A Chopping Expert

Neatly Slices And Packs Brother Away In Freezer

A Spanish butcher who cut up his own brother and stored the parts in his fridge-freezer next to his food has been caught after he turned himself in to the police.

Aurele Almanza, 48, claims to have killed his brother Osmas, 52, 'in self-defence', before slicing the body into pieces, neatly packing them away in freezer bags to escape arrest.

Mr Almanza's crime went undetected for a whole year before he confessed to local police on the Balearic Island of Mallorca.

Extreme sibling rivalry: Police open a chest freezer at the home of butcher Aurele Almanza, 48, in Palma de Mallorca, Mallorca, to find parts of his brother whom he killed a year ago

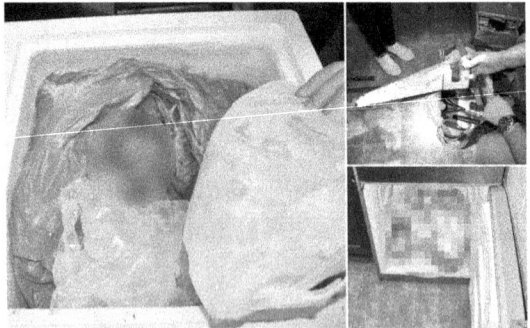

When police visited Mr Almanza's house in the island's capital of Palma de Mallorca, they found the body expertly chopped up and the parts stored in a chest freezer.

Gruesome Discovery

The second gruesome discovery came when they opened his kitchen fridge-freezer, finding that he had stored his brother's head and other parts below shelves filled with fresh food.

Mr Almanza claims he murdered his brother after Osmas had tried to attack him with a hammer during a fight,

Almanza said he had offered his brother a place to stay when he fell on hard times, but that they had frequently argued, escalating into a physical attack ending in Osmas's death.

"Are your chops humanely chopped?"

Mr Almanza claims his brother attacked him with a hammer after which he killed him in self-defence and cut him into pieces

He claims that he only killed his brother in self defence upon the hammer attack, and then had sliced up the body when he realised what he had done.

Finally, after keeping his brother's head in his kitchen fridge for more than a year, he claims is 'became too much' forcing him to hand himself in.

Source
Sara Malm, The Daily Mail, 1 October 2013
Capital Bay, Staff Writer, 09/30/2013

18

Animals Feel Just Like We Do

When We Will Understand This, All Wars Will End

Life Lessons From A Bull

After 25 years of working in slaughterhouses, Peter Razpet, from Kamnik in Slovenia, experienced an intense spiritual change which made him put down the butcher's knife forever. Here is his compelling interview for the Abolitionist-Online.

Peter: When I was a child my catholic parents registered me in Sunday Christian school. There they taught us that only humans had soul and feelings, animals however were second class beings, serving us, helping us at our work and being our food, but they had no soul and did not suffer like humans.

We had a bull at home. My father once beat him up right there in front of me and the animal started to hate him. My education prevented me from understanding where did all that hatred come from. My father didn't dare to get near the bull from that day on, so we had to sell him. I was the only one, who could pat him and talk to him, as if I was trying to beg him to forgive

my Dad. I always loved my father although he sometimes beat me up too. I still feel his kindness and love. He was my great teacher. Later, I never hit my children, because I knew, how badly it hurt.

When we sold the bull, butchers came to pick him up him with a truck. I felt sorry for him so I withdrew. But the bull would let none near him. So my father asked me to help them. I patted him and told him to be good, so I could take him to the truck. I untied him, told him once again I loved him and he followed me around like a puppy. When I bid him goodbye I saw tears in his eyes. I didn't understand it then. Now, as I write this, tears come to my eyes and I feel sorry I didn't understand then.

Now I know that animals have soul too, they feel the pain, love us maybe more than we love ourselves and others. They want to tell us something, teach us something, just as that bull tried to teach

The cows on our Hare Krsna farms are giving more milk than other cows--because they are confident, "We will not be killed here." It is not like these rascals, these so-called Christians, say: "They have no soul; they have no intelligence." They have intelligence. In other places they do not give so much milk. But on our farms they are very jolly. As soon as the devotees call, they'll come. Yes--just like friends. And they are confident, "We'll not be killed." So they are jubilant, and they are giving much milk. Yes.

In Europe and America the cows are very good, but the cow-killing system is also very good. So you stop this. You simply request them, "You'll get the cow's flesh. As soon as she is dead, we shall supply you free of charge. You haven't got to pay so much money. You can get the flesh free and eat it then. Why are you killing? Stop these slaughterhouses." What is wrong with this proposal?

We don't want to stop trade or the production of grains and vegetables and fruit. But we want to stop these killing houses. It is very, very sinful. That is why all over the world they have so many wars. Every ten or fifteen years there is a big war--a wholesale slaughterhouse for humankind. But these rascals--they do not see it, that by the law of karma, every action must have its reaction.

~ Srila Prabhupada (Conversation - Valencey, France, June 1974)

me. Thank God I didn't understand it then. If I did, I wouldn't be being interviewed now. I am glad I didn't have to kill him then. I would have killed someone who loved me and woke up my feelings. I am glad we parted as friends, but his tears will never be forgotten. They had their meaning.

"I WON'T BE LONG. HE'S GOING TO SHOW ME WHERE THEY MAKE HAMBURGERS."

I know now that he was trying to tell me:

Good bye my friend! Tell your Dad, the butchers and all other people, that animals don't hate, but we know how to forgive, so don't kill us without reason. Let us live, so we can all experience heaven, which is celebrated by high officials of the holy church. Finally understand, that the words 'do not kill' are meant for us too. When you understand it, like you did dear Peter, then all wars will end. There will be no more hunger, poor and rich people. Then everybody will have everything and you will all live together in love. Therefore don't judge, what you don't understand, don't judge those, who don't understand it, but help them by your example!

When the butchers saw how the bull followed me they suggested that I should start work as a butcher. And so I soon found myself in a slaughterhouse.

Some rascals put forward the theory that an animal has no soul or is something like dead stone. In this way they rationalize that there is no sin in animal killing. Actually animals are not dead stone, but the killers of animals are stone-hearted. Consequently no reason or philosophy appeals to them. They continue keeping slaughterhouses and killing animals.
-Srila Prabhupada (Srimad-Bhagavatam 4.26.9)

Source:

Peter Razpet Alvador, P.P. 36, 1241 Kamnik, Slovenija

Abolitionist-Online.com

Confessions of An Ex-Slaughterman, All-creatures.org

19

Man

The King of the carnivores

The world has a burgeoning appetite for meat. Fifty years ago global consumption was 70m tonnes. By 2007 it had risen to 268m tonnes.

In a similar vein, the amount of meat eaten by each person has leapt from around 22kg in 1961 to 40kg in 2007. Tastes have changed at the same time. Cow (beef and veal) was top of the menu

Why should man not be satisfied with grains, fruits and milk, which, combined together, can produce hundreds and thousands of palatable dishes. Why are there slaughterhouses all over the world to kill innocent animals? Maharaja Pariksit, grandson of Maharaja Yudhisthira, while touring his vast kingdom, saw a black man attempting to kill a cow. The King at once arrested the butcher and chastised him sufficiently. Should not a king or executive head protect the lives of the poor animals who are unable to defend themselves? Is this humanity? Are not the animals of a country citizens also? Then why are they allowed to be butchered in organized slaughterhouses? Are these the signs of equality, fraternity and nonviolence?

Therefore, in contrast with the modern, advanced, civilized form of government, an autocracy like Maharaja Yudhisthira's is by far superior to a so-called democracy in which animals are killed and a man less than an animal is allowed to cast votes for another less-than-animal man.

~ Srila Prabhupada (Srimad Bhagavatam 1.10.4 purport)

in the early 1960s, accounting for 40% of meat consumption, but by 2007 its share had fallen to 23%. Pig is now the animal of choice, with around 99m tonnes consumed.

Meanwhile advances in battery farming and health-related changes in Western diets have helped propel poultry from 12% to 31% of the global total.

Although populous middle-income countries such as China are driving the worldwide demand for meat, it is mainly Western countries who still eat most per person. Luxembourgers, who top this chart, are second only to Argentinians in beef consumption. Austrians are the keenest pig-eaters, wolfing down 66kg every year—just more than Serbians, Spaniards and even neighbouring Germans. At the other end of the scale, cow-revering Indians eat only 3.2kg of meat each, the least of the 177 countries assessed.

Source

The Economist, Apr 30th 2012, 'Who Eats Most Meat? Vegetarians Should Look Away'

Gary L. Francione: The Abolitionist Approach to Animal Rights

May 5, 2012

20

Cow - A Journey

From The Farm To Dinner Plate

The black and-white steer confined in the slaughterhouse killing chute is called an Angus, which is the name of the Celtic god of love. He weighs about 1,100 pounds and has lived his entire life of 19 months on a farm. As the slaughterer approaches him, he begins to move from the left to the right — and back again — on his front legs, and — if his facial expression can be translated into human terms — we would say he is terrified.

The slaughterer places a round stun gun at a point between and three inches above the steer's blinking eyes and fires a blank cartridge (bullets are not used because the steer's brain will later be sold for human consumption). The steer drops immediately and soundlessly to the floor.

"HE ALWAYS GETS THAT WAY WHEN I ASK HIM ABOUT OUR RETIREMENT PLAN."

The metamorphosis of living animal to cellophaned meat has begun.

The steer's two rear legs are brought together and fastened to a chain hoist. This is done with considerable difficulty, however, because the steer, though silent and glassy eyed, is still kicking and thrashing in frantic death throes. Once the chain is secured to the animal's leg, he is hauled upward so that he is hanging head-first over a six-foot-square concrete pit.

The steer vomits into the pit while the slaughterer sharpens a long knife and then, in one quick motion, slits the animal's throat. Blood pours into the pit like running water from a hose. The blood pours in a steady stream for several minutes and fills the pit to about three inches. At some unknown point, the steer bleeds to death.

There is no sound in the hollow room except for a radio, which is playing gospel music, and the air is thick with the smell of blood and decaying flesh.

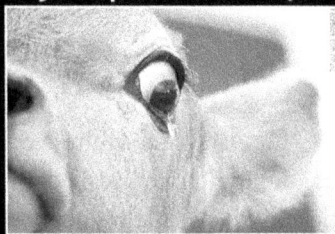

If you think eating meat is just a personal choice,

You are forgetting someone.

The slaughterer wears high rubber boots and a rubber apron, which are frequently hosed off to remove blood. Blood covers his hands and arms, and it is splattered on his neck and face. He steps into the steaming pool of warm blood and beheads the steer. Holding it by one of its horns, he carries the dripping head to a barrel, where he deposits it with the heads of other cattle. The headless carcass

To be nonviolent to human beings and to be a killer or enemy of the poor animals is Satan's philosophy. In this age there is enmity toward poor animals, and therefore the poor creatures are always anxious. The reaction of the poor animals is being forced on human society, and therefore there is always the strain of cold or hot war between men, individually, collectively or nationally.

—Srila Prabhupada Srimad Bhagavatam 1.10.6

is removed to a low-lying metal block, called a cradle, where two other workers lay it on its back. Its legs, which are sticking upward, are severed and the steer is neatly skinned, rear to front.

The animal is eviscerated and its unsalable entrails are removed and hung separately — livers with livers, hearts with hearts, tails with tails, tongues with tongues. The men work quickly and with the same robot-like mannerisms that munitions workers develop around dynamite. The slaughterers frequently stop to hose themselves and their work area. Meanwhile, the original slaughterer is using a squeeze mop to push the blood into the concrete pit and down a small drain.

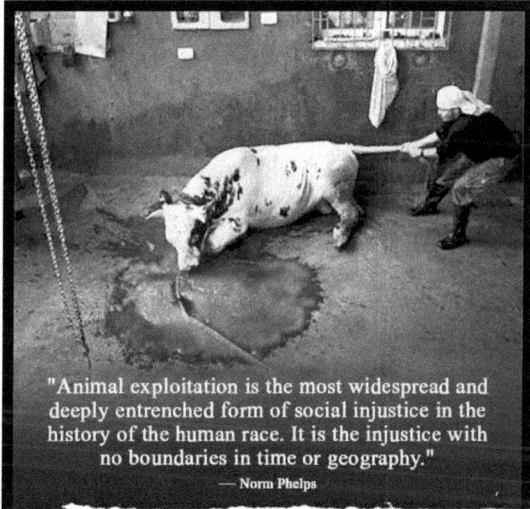

"Animal exploitation is the most widespread and deeply entrenched form of social injustice in the history of the human race. It is the injustice with no boundaries in time or geography."
— Norm Phelps

The skinless, headless carcass is again hoisted up on a mechanical pulley and, beginning between the rear legs, a worker with a huge power saw cuts it in half. The resulting two sides of beef are hosed clean of blood and hung in a refrigerated room. Later, the halves will be butchered and given names like brisket, sirloin, prime rib, rump, round, shank, flank and chuck.

The 1,100-pound animal will yield about 600 pounds of meat. Each piece will be weighed, priced, placed on a styrofoam tray and wrapped in cellophane. Humans will buy these pieces of flesh, and then broil, sauté, fry, bake or grill them until the meat develops a third-degree burn. After a scab has formed on the meat, humans will call them "crispy" — and then eat them.

Source

Glass Walls, Suzana Margaret Megles

Grandin, T. "Best Practices for Animal Handling and Stunning"", Meat & Poultry, April 2000

Muhlke, Christine (23 May 2010). "Field Report; A Movable Beast". The New York Times.

21

A Scream Is Much The Same

Whatever The Species That Utters It

A Childhood Memory, Paulette Callen

The stench. Why did my mother bring me here? Oh, yes...she had a message for somebody who worked here. I walked by this strangely shaped grey building with no windows every day on my way to and from school. A building without windows. What kind of building doesn't have windows?

Sometimes I heard sounds coming from inside. Muffled. High-pitched. Like people screaming. But it couldn't be. I was old enough to know that just couldn't be. Nothing bad could be happening in there. It wouldn't be allowed. I was old enough to know that. So I passed the building each morning and evening with a strange prickling of dread, and forgot about it till the next time.

Until that day my mother took me inside. The place was thick with a reeking steam that rose out of a cauldron gurgling and frothing with oily brown bubbles. The smell. Feces. Urine. I was sorting out the smells — rather, my brain was sorting them by itself. I was trying to block them out. Something was being hauled out of the cauldron, either on a rope or belt, or maybe giant pincers, I couldn't tell. It was up and out and swung off to the side out of my line of vision.

The smell. Blood. Old, standing, congealing, rotting blood mingled with the warm metallic smell of flesh. I could see blood now, on the floor oozing from a place where I couldn't see. The man talking to my mother was wearing high rubber boots and a rubber apron, all spattered with slime.

The smells. Singed flesh and hair and something else...now what was happening?

A door slid open with a soft woosh of wood on wood. I looked down into the seething cauldron. The chute was slick with brown and yellow excrement...what?...a pig was shoved through the door onto a dock and poised there, just blinking. He was pink and brown and seemed to shine above the muck he looked down upon. I thought: He is smelling the same things I am.

A man on a platform above whacked the pig across the forehead with a large rod of some kind, but he didn't go down. He wasn't dead. He wasn't even stunned and he began to scream before he fell. His knees buckled, in fear, I think, not from the blow, and he slid down the chute screaming. Screaming.

I understand that we're all on a journey in life, we all have different likes and dislikes, different nationalities and religions too, but there's one thing that we need to have in common with each other and that's peace, genuine compassion and genuine peace for our planetary companions. Contrary to political and religious dogma, animals do not belong to us. They are not commodities. They're not property and they're not inanimate stupid objects that can't think and feel. That Cartesian way of looking at animals like they're machines is out-dated and quite frankly, 100% insane...
~Gary Yourofsky

Scream - The Sound of Being In Pain

A scream, I have observed since, is much the same, whatever the species that utters it.

A scream born of terror: the sound of Being, in pain.

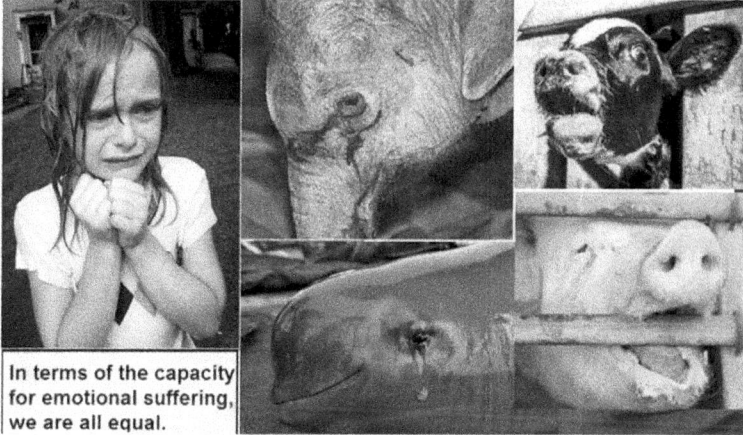

In terms of the capacity for emotional suffering, we are all equal.

I've heard a cat scream and it sounded just like a child. A horse that sounded like a man. A man who sounded like — one of his compatriots said at the time — "like a stuck pig." It's all the same.

The pig, screaming, slid down the chute into the cauldron of boiling muck. He didn't stop screaming till the muck closed over

Regardless of whether human, animal, tree or plant, all living entities are sons of the Supreme Personality of Godhead. Lord Krsna says in Bhagavad-gita (14.4):

sarva-yonisu kaunteya
murtayah sambhavanti yah
tasam brahma mahad yonir
aham bija-pradah pita

"It should be understood that all species of life, O son of Kunti, are made possible by birth in this material nature, and that I am the seed-giving father."

—Srila Prabhupada

his head. In a moment he, too, was lifted out and another creature stood blinking and shining at the top of the chute.

I staggered out of the slaughterhouse and leaned against the back wall, vomiting. My mother found me. "What's the matter, Honey? Have an upset stomach? Here." She handed me her handkerchief. It was trimmed with ecru lace. "Let's go home and settle your stomach. You'll probably feel better after you've had something to eat."

Source
"A Childhood Memory", Paulette Callen

22

South Korea - Burying Alive Millions

Insanity or cruelty?

By Kim Heung-sook

I often wake up in the middle of the night these days and hear the imaginary cries of cattle and pigs. "Help us!" They scream but there is nothing I can do to save them. The nation has buried 1.4 million cows and pigs alive for the prevention of foot-and-mouth disease. Anyone who can sleep well while the animals struggle for life underground should be either cold-hearted or extremely overworked.

In my childhood, my family lived in the port city of Gunsan on the west coast. Every winter, the whole city turned into a white canvas of snow on which everyone left marks of one's own. The most striking was the red dots left by bicycles carrying fresh beef and pork from the slaughterhouse. Adults banned children from entering the red brick house and its precincts for obvious reasons, but we went there anyway.

It was in the 1960s and we didn't have any factory farms in Korea. Cattle were taken to slaughterhouses after working through their lifetime, while pigs came from small family pens. While pigs entered into the compound noisily, cows usually refused to come in at the main gate. People whispered that cows knew they were doomed. When cows resisted at the gate, their original owners, who were farmers, were summoned. They would caress and coax the animals and the latter walked into the brick house without further ado.

One day, I saw a farmer lead a cow into the house. He let the cow stand on a cemented podium. He rubbed her cheek with his chestnut hands. Then a man with an axe appeared from behind and planted it on top of the cow's head. The animal collapsed with a thump and it echoed forever. That was the first and most impressive scene of betrayal and death I have observed in my whole life. I saw the teary eyes of the farmer, yet I couldn't forgive him for what he had done to the unsuspecting animal.

It was much later that I came to remember the scene of death with less remorse and some inexplicable warmth. While the cattle were destined to die at the slaughterhouse, people cared about their feelings. There was a proper ritual of parting and expression of appreciation and sorrow that spared the victim unnecessary pains.

All other living entities think like yourself. That means your pains and pleasure that you feel, you should take others pains and pleasure. Not that you protect yourself from all danger and you cut the throat of the poor animals on the plea that it has no soul. This is not education. This is education, that whether the animal has soul or not soul, we shall consider later on. But when knife is on my throat I cry, and he also cries. Why shall I say that it has no soul and let me kill it?
—Srila Prabhupada (Lecture, Honolulu, May 22, 1976)

At that time, we ate beef and pork only on festive days like Chuseok and Seollal, and birthdays and death anniversaries of ancestors. There were few fat people though the word diet was never heard of. Our stomachs were not full most of the time, yet we shared whatever we came by. We believed we should share even a single bean.

As the nation became richer, demand for meat grew. In 2008, the per capita meat consumption of Koreans topped 35.4 kg, more than three times the volume consumed in 1983. To meet the ever-growing appetite for meat, factory farming was introduced for beef, pork and poultry. Now, people eat meat all year round, constantly worrying about gaining weight. The Korean characteristic has also changed from "quiet tenacity" to "palli palli" or "faster and faster."

People buy beef, pork and poultry from supermarkets as they buy milk, cookies and Kleenex; they are oblivious to the creatures that provide their flesh. Few care about how they live and die. The government's burial of 1.4 million cattle and pigs since November showcases the widespread apathy towards the meat providers.

The government says the burial is for preventive purposes but the measure had already proved futile. Since FMD was first reported in

Ask any working class person over 50-60 what they used to eat as a child, and they will confirm that it was only possible to eat a small amount of meat, except on special occasions. I am Over 50, a working class raised dude here.

Meat was indeed far more a luxury item than it is nowadays. Unfortunately my grandad was an agricultural builder and used to quite often get part paid in dead piggies that had neatly been bandsawed in half, from food inlet to food outlet, right through the middle.

Nothing was wasted though. From trotters to ears, and all in bits between, every scrap got eaten. Even the skulls were boiled to get every last scrap of flesh off (made 'brawn') and the bones boiled in broth to extract every last morsel of marrow.

Somehow in those days meat eating was far more .... 'respectful' and 'honest'.

~ Ian Birrell, Colorado

late November in Andong, North Gyeongsang Province, preventive killing was done near and far, yet the disease spread to Gyeonggi and Chungcheong Provinces. Still, the massive killing continues in the name of prevention. The government is insane and/or cruel, if not plain incapable.

If humans are not affected by FMD and even infected meat is safe for human consumption as the health authorities say, why does the government keep on burying these animals to death? Can't they be taken to the proper facilities and be killed by electric shock or other means causing minimum pain?

As many of the farmers and officials involved in the livestock massacre are suffering from symptoms of post-traumatic stress disorder (PTSD), the Ministry of Health and Welfare has decided to offer counseling and treatment through the 158 mental health centers across the country. The sufferers are humane to say the least. If people bury over a million innocent animals alive and feel unperturbed, they can't be humans, can they? I wonder if the high-ranking officials who ordered the burial of the livestock have ever been to the hell they are creating down there. If they haven't, they need to go there once and for all.

Source
The Korea Times, January 14, 2011, Kim Heung-sook
The Korea Herald, Jan 23, 2011.

antar dehesu bhutanam
atmaste harir isvarah
sarvam tad-dhisnyam iksadhvam
evam vas tosito hy asau
The Supreme Personality of Godhead is situated as the Supersoul within the cores of the hearts of all living entities, whether moving or nonmoving, including men, birds, animals, trees and, indeed, all living entities. Therefore you should consider every body a residence or temple of the Lord. By such vision you will satisfy the Lord.
- Srimad Bhagavatam 6.4.13

23

A Town Turns Into A Slaughterhouse

Srebrenica: Worst European Atrocity Since WWII

Srebrenica is a town and municipality in the east of Bosnia and Herzegovina. Srebrenica is a small mountain town, its main industry being salt mining and a nearby spa.

During the Bosnian War, the town was the site of a July 1995 massacre, determined to have been a crime of genocide.

It is now remembered as the worst atrocity in Europe since World War II.

In a five-day orgy of slaughter at Srebrenica in July 1995, up to 8,000 Bosniak Muslims were systematically exterminated in what

was described at the U.N. war crimes tribunal as "the triumph of evil."

Former Bosnian Serb commander-in-chief General Ratko Mladic, who is accused of direct involvement in the genocide at Srebrenica, was arrested after more than 15 years on the run.

In 1995, Srebrenica was designated a U.N. "safe area."

A judge at The Hague tribunal was later to describe what happened there as "truly scenes from hell written on the darkest pages of human history."

Thousands of Bosnian Muslims had sought refuge in the spa town of Srebrenica in 1995 as the Bosnian Serb army marched towards them.

They were protected by just 100 lightly equipped Dutch peacekeepers -- who proved no match for the advancing, heavily-armed Serb army.

Denied reinforcements, the Dutch were forced to stand aside while Serb troops intent on "ethnic cleansing" did their worst -- the peacekeepers even witnessing the summary execution of civilians.

In the days before the onslaught, 30,000 Muslims fleeing the advancing Serb army were crammed into the town. Within days there was not one Muslim left.

A great number fled -- only for many of them to be wiped out in Serb ambushes -- but the men who stayed fared the worst.

Thousands of men and boys as young as 10 were rounded up and murdered. Those who tried to hide in their homes were, according to evidence at the trial of Serb General Radislav Krstic at The Hague in March 2000, "hunted down like dogs and slaughtered."

Serbian TV footage shows women and children being separated from the men and put on buses.

In a sickening show of "reassurance" Mladic -- now on the war crimes tribunal's most wanted list -- told the women everyone would be taken out by bus out and safely reunited.

In your Christian religion also, it is clearly stated, "Thou shall not kill." But who is caring for that? Nobody is caring. They are killing. That killing process is increasing, and there is reaction also. Every ten years you will find one war, killing process upon you. How you can avoid? There must be reaction. You cannot violate the laws of God. As you cannot violate the laws of the state, similarly, if you violate, you have to suffer. You cannot expect peace and you go on killing animals. That is not possible. If you want peace, then you must think for others also. That is Krsna consciousness. That is God consciousness. How you can kill another animal? He is also as good a child of God.

A father has got some dozens of children. It may be one is useless, but that does not mean father will allow it to be killed, allow him to be killed. If the very intelligent child says, "My dear father, your this son is useless. Let me kill him." The father will sanction? No, never. Similarly, the animal may be less intelligent. They cannot make protest. They are also nationals. What do you mean by national? One who is born in America is national. Are the animals are not born in America? Are they not American nationals? But because they cannot make protest, they cannot make meeting, you are killing them. You see? Is that humanity? And you expect peace? That is not possible. Violation of God, laws of God. One has to suffer, today or tomorrow. Today or tomorrow.

~ Srila Prabhupada (Bhagavad-gita 4.7-10 -- Los Angeles, January 6, 1969)

When the cameras were turned off the real face of the Serb army emerged as the slaughter began.

More than 60 truckloads of refugees were taken from Srebrenica to execution sites where they were bound, blindfolded, and shot with automatic rifles.

Some of the executions were carried out at night under arc lights. Industrial bulldozers then pushed the bodies into mass graves.

Some were buried alive, a French policeman who collected evidence from Bosnian Muslims, Jean-Rene Ruez, told The Hague tribunal in 1996.

He gave evidence that Bosnian Serb forces had killed and tortured refugees at will. Streets were littered with corpses, he said, and rivers were red with blood. Many people committed suicide to avoid having their noses, lips and ears chopped off, he said.

Among other lurid accounts of mass murder, Ruez cited cases of adults being forced to kill their children or watching as soldiers ended the young lives.

"One soldier approached a woman in the middle of a crowd," he said. "Her child was crying. The soldier asked why the child was crying and she explained that he was hungry. The soldier made a comment like, 'He won't be hungry anymore.' He slit the child's throat in front of everybody."

Source
Graham Jones, CNN, July 3, 2006
Srebrenica's yearly burial of atrocity victims". Euronews. 11 July 2012
The United Nations' Report on The Fall of Srebrenica (1999)

24

Story of Hyenas

2 Legged And 4 Legged

Throwaway Lives: The Massacre Of Pregnant Animals

This was the devastating moment a heavily pregnant zebra was killed by hyenas in Africa.

It was a scene that photographer Marc Mol found incredibly difficult to watch – other onlookers couldn't bear it and left.

The harrowing scene unfolded in Kenya's Maasai Mara National Reserve in Narok County, with the mare set upon by 20 hyenas.

The zebra looked on in a stoic and defiant manner as the animals attacked.

Wildlife photographer Mr Mol revealed that the zebra's misery lasted for 20 minutes.

Mr Mol said: 'It was one of the most remarkable events I've ever seen.

'My wife and I observed this predation by a pack of hyenas on this poor and unfortunate Zebra mare who was heavily pregnant and simply couldn't keep up with the herd.

'It was the first time my guide of 15 years and I had ever witnessed something like this.

'Subsequently the unborn foal was savagely ripped out and carried off by one of the hyenas.

'It was absolutely heart-breaking to watch, simply too much for one person in another vehicle next to us and they left after this happened.

'Throughout the attack, the mare didn't utter a sound as the savagery of the pack set in, no doubt in severe shock.

'It was not an easy event to photograph and document as I witnessed two lives being taken, but this is after all the struggle for survival in the circle of life.'

Mr Mol also revealed that one hyena made off with the unborn foal and a black-backed jackal stole some of its kill.

Killing Pregnant Animals And Throwing Away Unborn Babies

- A British Case Study

This was an isolated case of 4 legged hyenas killing a pregnant mare in Maasai Mara but 2 legged hyenas are even worse. They brutally kill pregnant animals every day.

How Many Pregnant Animals Are Killed In Britain?

DEFRA (Department of Environment, Food & Rural Affairs) say that they do not see any justification for recording the number of pregnant animals who are slaughtered. However, a scientific paper published by the British Cattle Veterinary Association reveals that 150,000 pregnant cows are sent to slaughter each year. At least 40,000 of these cows are in the last stages of their pregnancy and are bearing calves who are capable of independent life.

Why are pregnant cows being killed?

90% of the cows are dairy cows and the majority of farmers do not even realize that they are pregnant. In the BCVA survey, 50.9% thought the cow wasn't pregnant and 27.3% said they did not know. Infertility was cited as the most common reason for culling an animal, followed by mastitis (a painful swelling of the udders common in dairy cows) and then old age. So some cows are being sent to slaughter because they are assumed to be infertile when they are in fact pregnant. Dairy cows who are over thirty months of age must be slaughtered and incinerated under BSE regulations. The compensation payment structure encourages the killing of pregnant cows. Animals sent through market are weighed liveweight and the farmer is compensated per kilo. If the animal is pregnant, the farmer will receive extra money.

How are the animals killed?

There are no special regulations in place to protect pregnant animals in slaughterhouses. Viva! has filmed in abattoirs and

Gabriele Meurer MRCVS, a former official veterinary surgeon in UK abattoirs, says, "What is happening right now in British slaughterhouses is quite simply a scandal. Sometimes when these creatures are hanging on the line bleeding to death, you can see the unborn calves kicking inside their mothers' wombs. I, as a vet, am not supposed to do anything about this. Unborn calves do not exist according to the regulations. I just had to watch, do nothing and keep quiet. It broke my heart. I felt like a criminal. I left the Meat Hygiene Service and the country - completely disillusioned and full of disgust."

conducted a full investigation of the UK's slaughter industry. They found that stunning techniques are frequently inadequate and that animals routinely regain consciousness whilst bleeding to death.

Each year, 5 million electrically stunned sheep regain consciousness before they die from loss of blood.

1.8 million electrically stunned pigs a year regain consciousness before they die. 244,800 pigs a year are incorrectly stunned and do not lose consciousness at all.

Each year, up to 230,000 cattle are not correctly stunned with the captive bolt pistol. They will have to endure the pain of being shot in the head and will then have to be shot again or knifed whilst conscious.

Do unborn animals suffer as their mothers are slaughtered?

The RSPCA's chief veterinary officer states, "The problem with killing heavily pregnant ewes is that if you shoot them in the head, the foetus does not die instantly with the mother and it is a prolonged and rather horrible death."

After animals have been stunned, they are knifed and left to bleed out for 20 seconds (sheep and pigs) or 30 seconds (cattle). When asked about the slaughter of pregnant cows, Professor Donald Broom (Cambridge university animal welfare specialist) said, "After stunning and bleeding the cow will be dead. The calf will also die but a little later - probably 30-90 seconds" . This means that the

Is there legislation in place to protect pregnant animals and unborn babies?

Animals are not supposed to be transported if they are likely to give birth during transport. However, Viva! campaigners have filmed animals giving birth at market when they were about to be loaded up for the slaughterhouse. The BCVA paper also shows that pregnant cows are frequently slaughtered in the third trimester of their pregnancy.

There is no legislation to protect unborn animals in abattoirs - even if they are days away from being born.

foetus would still be living while its mother's front feet, head and possibly hide are removed.

Nobody is sure of the exact moment when foetuses die. It is possible that they may still be living when the mother is disembowelled.

Christopher Day MRCVS says, "The routine slaughter of known pregnant animals in the UK should be made illegal forthwith, on humane grounds. In this country we make pretensions to be compassionate to animals. This practice is wholly inconsistent with such pretensions."

What happens to the foetus?

DEFRA says that, "The uterus and dead foetus is sent with the green offal from the slaughterhouse for disposal by rendering from any pregnant animals which are under thirty months when slaughtered. All material from animals over thirty months (which is the majority of cows slaughtered) has to be separated, stained yellow and destroyed by rendering and incineration."

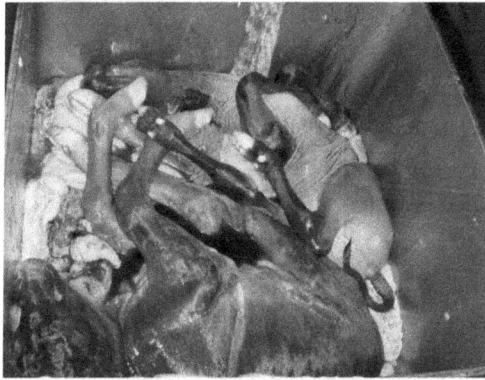

Calf fetuses at an abattoir. Many cows are pregnant at their time of slaughter. This is the bin where unborn calves are discarded when they are cut out while the mother is butchered. They lay wet with their hooves still soft and are still attached to their placentas. In addition to the trauma of still being alive inside their mothers during the latter's death, fetal calves may also be cut from their mother's womb while still alive--so that their blood can be drained for use in science, without anesthesia (fetal bovine serum or fetal calf serum) - the calf's skin is used to make 'high quality' leather.

Is the government doing anything to stop the slaughter?

When Viva! asked what the government planned to do to prevent so many pregnant cows from being sent to slaughter, DEFRA replied, "We do not believe that the slaughter of pregnant cows presents a specific welfare concern...We do not believe further legal measures are necessary to protect the welfare of pregnant cows or unborn calves."

However, they say that, "Effective pregnancy detection lessens the risk of inadvertently sending pregnant animals for slaughter".The department is currently consulting on proposals to change the law to allow 'per rectum' ultrasound scanning in cattle to be carried out by, "trained and competent non-veterinarians as well as by veterinary surgeons."

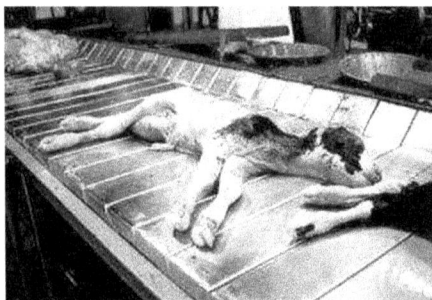

DEFRA has been consulting on these proposals for over three years. Consultation papers reveal that, "Concern has been expressed by the veterinary profession and some animal protection societies that use of this procedure by untrained non-veterinarians to detect pregnancy in cattle could cause welfare problems. Invasive

He visited a gas chamber, outside which he signed a book of condolence for the victims. Mr Cameron wrote: 'I wanted to come and see for myself this place where the darkest chapter of human history happened.

'Words cannot describe the horror that took place – making it even more important that we never forget.'

He added: 'As Elie Wiesel said, failing to remember those who were murdered would be akin to failing them all over again.

'The survivors here have so much to tell us about what took place. Today they are becoming fewer in number so I hope the Holocaust Commission we have established will teach future generations what took place and that we must never forget all those who were murdered here and at other camps and in other places.

'We must always remember what happened.'

techniques of this nature have the potential to cause serious injury, such as perforation of the rectal wall."

Mr. Prime Minister! Auschwitz Camps Exist Right In Your Own Country

David Cameron, the British Prime Minister, lit a candle in memory of the millions of Holocaust victims as he made his first visit to the Auschwitz concentration camp.

The Prime Minister said he wanted to come to the site to see for himself where the 'darkest chapter of human history' took place.

And he said: 'We must never forget all those who were murdered here'.

Mr Cameron honoured a pledge made last year to tour the camp in Poland, where more than a million died at the hands of the Nazi regime.

The Prime Minister spent more than an hour in the two main camps which make up the site. Mr Cameron said: 'It is a reminder of why the UK must fight against prejudice, persecution, anti-semitism and tyranny wherever we find it and stand up for inclusiveness, tolerance and peace.'

Mr Cameron made the trip on the way back from a visit to Turkey, where he met political leaders to discuss the threat from Islamic State militants.

Around one and a half million men, women and children were killed - 90 per cent of them Jewish - in Auschwitz when the area was occupied by the Nazis during the Second World War.

The site, which was liberated by the Red Army in 1945, is a network of concentration camps and extermination camps.

"What is your definition of holocaust? Is it a massacre of humanbeings, or a massacre of innocent beings? In America alone we murder10 billion land animals and 18 billion marine animals every year. Not for health, survival, sustenance, or self-defense - people eat meat, cheese, milk and eggs for 4 reasons: habit, tradition, convenience, and taste...
  ~Gary Yourofsky

Prisoners were also used as slave labour, as cruelly depicted by the 'Arbeit Macht Frei' sign which Mr Cameron viewed at the main Auschwitz I site.

On a bitterly cold day, the Prime Minister visited the neighbouring Birkenau camp where he saw the train line on which Jewish prisoners arrived before being incarcerated.

And he paid his respects at a memorial to the victims - lighting a candle and pausing in silent reflection.

Mick Davis, chairman of the Holocaust Commission, who accompanied Mr Cameron, said 'you only begin to understand the enormity of the Holocaust and the huge impact on humanity' by visiting the camp.

> *Right now at this very moment on American highways there are no less than 5,000 concentration camp trucks - trucks that we've constructed. Inside these trucks there are living, terrified, innocent beings. These trucks are being driven to concentration camp slaughterhouses that we've carefully constructed all across America. When the trucks arrive the animals are so frightened they won't even get off the truck. They're not stupid. They know what's next. So people go on the trucks with electric prods and force them to walk down the chutes to their own deaths...*
> *~Gary Yourofsky*

'I was just speaking to the Prime Minister just before he left for the airport, and he said to me that he's looked at all the films and read the books but you just can't understand the scale of what happened - the deprivation that took place, the collapse of humanity,' he said.

'Being here was important to the understanding of what took place.'

Mr Davis said he was worried that as survivors of the Holocaust passed away, 'society has a habit of consigning history to books and sterility'.

Mr Cameron promised last year to visit Auschwitz during 2014. He said at the time of the pledge that more must be done to preserve the memory of the Holocaust at a time when 'anti-Semitism is returning to some parts of Europe'.

The Prime Minister announced an increase in government funding for the Holocaust Educational Trust, which takes children and teachers to visit Auschwitz-Birkenau.

Source
Ted Thornhill, The Daily Mail, 3 April 2014
Daniel Martin, The Daily Mail, 10 December 2014
BBC, 10 December 2014
Auschwitz-Birkenau, Then And Now 27 February 2012

25

Animals Are Other Nations

And The Peace Map Is Drawn On A Menu

King Lear, late at night on the cliffs asks the blind Earl of Gloucester "How do you see the world?"

And the blind man Gloucester replies "I see it feelingly".

Shouldn't we all?

Animals must be off the menu because tonight they are screaming in terror in the slaughterhouse, in crates, and cages. Vile ignoble gulags of despair.

I heard the screams of my dying father as his body was ravaged by the cancer that killed him. And I realised I had heard these screams before.

In the slaughterhouse, eyes stabbed out and tendons slashed, on the cattle ships to the Middle East and the dying mother whale as a Japanese harpoon explodes in her brain as she calls out to her calf.

Their cries were the cries of my father.

I discovered when we suffer, we suffer as equals.

And in their capacity to suffer, a dog is a pig is a bear......is a boy.

Meat is the new asbestos – more murderous than tobacco.

CO_2, Methane, and Nitrous Oxide from the livestock industry are killing our oceans with acidic, hypoxic Dead Zones.

90% of small fish are ground into pellets to feed livestock.

Vegetarian cows are now the world's largest ocean predator.

The oceans are dying in our time. By 2048 all our fisheries will be dead. The lungs and the arteries of the earth.

Billions of bouncy little chicks are ground up alive simply because they are male.

Only 100 billion people have ever lived. 7 billion alive today. And we torture and kill 2 billion animals every week.

10,000 entire species are wiped out every year because of the actions of one species.

We are now facing the 6th mass extinction in cosmological history.

If any other organism did this a biologist would call it a virus.

It is a crime against humanity of unimaginable proportions.

The world has changed.

10 years ago Twitter was a bird sound, www was a stuck keyboard, Cloud was in the sky, 4 g was a parking place, Google was a baby burp, Skype was a typo and Al Kider was my plumber.

Victor Hugo said "there is nothing more powerful than an idea whose time has come".

Animal Rights is now the greatest Social Justice issue since the abolition of slavery.

There are over 600 million vegetarians in the world.

That is bigger than the US, England, France, Germany, Spain, Italy, Canada, Australia combined! If we were one nation we would be bigger than the 27 countries in the European Union!!

Despite this massive footprint, we are still drowned out by the raucous huntin', shootin', killin' cartels who believe that violence is the answer – when it shouldn't even be a question.

Meat is a killing industry – animals, us and our economies.

Medicare has already bankrupted the US. They will need $8 trillion invested in Treasury bills just to pay the interest. It has precisely zero!!

They could shut every school, army, navy, air force, and Marines, the FBI and CIA – and they still won't be able to pay for it.

Cornell and Harvard say's that the optimum amount of meat for a healthy diet is precisely ZERO.

Water is the new oil. Nations will soon be going to war for it.

Underground aquifers that took millions of years to fill are running dry.

It takes 50,000 litres of water to produce one kilo of beef.

1 billion people today are hungry. 20 million people will die from malnutrition. Cutting meat by only 10% will feed 100 million people. Eliminating meat will end starvation forever.

If everyone ate a Western diet, we would need 2 Planet Earths to feed them. We only have one. And she is dying.

Greenhouse gas from livestock is 50% more than transport . . . . . planes, trains, trucks, cars, and ships.

Poor countries sell their grain to the West while their own children starve in their arms. And we feed it to livestock. So we can eat a steak? Am I the only one who sees this as a crime? Every morsel of meat we eat is slapping the tear-stained face of a starving child. When I look into her eyes, should I be silent?

The earth can produce enough for everyone's need. But not enough for everyone's greed.

We are facing the perfect storm.

If any nation had developed weapons that could wreak such havoc on the planet, we would launch a pre-emptive military strike and bomb it into the Bronze Age.

But it is not a rogue state. It is an industry.

The good news is we don't have to bomb it. We can just stop buying it.

George Bush was wrong. The Axis of Evil doesn't run through Iraq, or Iran or North Korea. It runs through our dining tables. Weapons of Mass Destruction are our knives and forks.

This is the Swiss Army Knife of the future – it solves our environmental, water, health problems and ends cruelty forever.

The Stone Age didn't end because we ran out of stones. This cruel industry will end because we run out of excuses.

Meat is like 1 and 2 cent coins. It costs more to make than it is worth.

And farmers are the ones with the most to gain. Farming won't end. It would boom. Only the product line would change. Farmers would make so much money they wouldn't even bother counting it.

Governments will love us. New industries would emerge and flourish. Health insurance premiums would plummet. Hospital

sarva-bhutesu yenaikam
bhavam avyayam iksate
avibhaktam vibhaktesu
taj jnanam viddhi sattvikam

That knowledge by which one undivided spiritual nature is seen in all living entities, though they are divided into innumerable forms, you should understand to be in the mode of goodness. (Bhagavad-gita 18.20)

A person who sees one spirit soul in every living being, whether a demigod, human being, animal, bird, beast, aquatic or plant, possesses knowledge in the mode of goodness. In all living entities, one spirit soul is there, although they have different bodies in terms of their previous work. As described in the Seventh Chapter, the manifestation of the living force in every body is due to the superior nature of the Supreme Lord. Thus to see that one superior nature, that living force, in every body is to see in the mode of goodness. That living energy is imperishable, although the bodies are perishable. Differences are perceived in terms of the body; because there are many forms of material existence in conditional life, the living force appears to be divided. Such impersonal knowledge is an aspect of self-realization.

—*Srila Prabhupada (Bhagavad-gita 18.20)*

waiting lists would disappear. Hell "We'd be so healthy; we'd have to shoot someone just to start a cemetery!"

So tonight I have 2 Challenges for the opposition:

1. Meat causes a wide range of cancers and heart disease. Will they name one disease caused by a vegetarian diet?

2. I am funding the Earthlings trilogy. If the opposition is so sure of their ground, I challenge them to send the Earthlings DVD to all their colleagues and customers. Go on I DARE YOU.

Animals are not just other species. They are other nations. And we murder them at our peril.

The peace map is drawn on a menu. Peace is not just the absence of war. It is the presence of Justice.

Justice must be blind to race, colour, religion or species. If she is not blind, she will be a weapon of terror. And there is unimaginable terror in those ghastly Guantanamos.

If slaughterhouses had glass walls, we wouldn't need this debate.

I believe another world is possible.

On a quiet night, I can hear her breathing.

Let's get the animals off the menu and out of these torture chambers.

Please vote tonight for those who have no voice.

Thank you.

Source
Philip Wollen, Australian Philanthropist, Former VP of Citibank,
Speech at the St James Ethics Centre on May 16, 2012.

26

Thou shalt not kill

All Life Is Sacred

At a monastic retreat near Paris, in July of 1973, Srila Prabhupada talked with Cardinal Jean Danielou: "... the Bible does not simply say, 'Do not kill the human being.' It says broadly, 'Thou shalt not kill.'... why do you interpret this to suit your own convenience?"

Srila Prabhupada: Jesus Christ said, "Thou shalt not kill." So why is it that the Christian people are engaged in animal killing?

Cardinal Danielou: Certainly in Christianity it is forbidden to kill, but we believe that there is a difference between the life of a human being and the life of the beasts. The life of a human being is sacred because man is made in the image of God; therefore, to kill a human being is forbidden.

Srila Prabhupada: But the Bible does not simply say, "Do not kill the human being." It says broadly, "Thou shalt not kill."

Cardinal Danielou: We believe that only human life is sacred.

Srila Prabhupada: That is your interpretation. The commandment is "Thou shalt not kill."

Cardinal Danielou: It is necessary for man to kill animals in order to have food to eat.

Srila Prabhupada: No. Man can eat grains, vegetables, fruits, and milk.

Cardinal Danielou: No flesh?

Srila Prabhupada: No. Human beings are meant to eat vegetarian food. The tiger does not come to eat your fruits. His prescribed food is animal flesh. But man's food is vegetables, fruits, grains, and milk products. So how can you say that animal killing is not a sin?

Cardinal Danielou: We believe it is a question of motivation. If the killing of an animal is for giving food to the hungry, then it is justified.

Srila Prabhupada: But consider the cow: we drink her milk; therefore, she is our mother. Do you agree?

Cardinal Danielou: Yes, surely.

Srila Prabhupada: So if the cow is your mother, how can you support killing her? You take the milk from her, and when she's old and cannot give you milk, you cut her throat. Is that a very humane proposal? In India those who are meat-eaters are advised to kill some lower animals like goats, pigs, or even buffalo. But cow killing is the greatest sin. In preaching Krsna consciousness we ask people not to eat any kind of meat, and my disciples strictly follow this principle. But if, under certain circumstances, others are obliged to eat meat, then they should eat the flesh of some lower animal. Don't kill cows. It is the greatest sin. And as long as a man is sinful, he cannot understand God. The human being's main business is to understand God and to love Him. But if you remain sinful, you will never be able to understand God--what to speak of loving Him.

Cardinal Danielou: I think that perhaps this is not an essential point. The important thing is to love God. The practical commandments can vary from one religion to the next.

Srila Prabhupada: So, in the Bible God's practical commandment is that you cannot kill; therefore killing cows is a sin for you.

Cardinal Danielou: God says to the Indians that killing is not good, and he says to the Jews that...

Srila Prabhupada: No, no. Jesus Christ taught, "Thou shalt not kill." Why do you interpret this to suit your own convenience?

Cardinal Danielou: But Jesus allowed the sacrifice of the Paschal Lamb.

Srila Prabhupada: But he never maintained a slaughterhouse.

Cardinal Danielou: [Laughs.] No, but he did eat meat.

Srila Prabhupada: When there is no other food, someone may eat meat in order to keep from starving. That is another thing. But it is most sinful to regularly maintain slaughterhouses just to satisfy your tongue. Actually, you will not even have a human society until this cruel practice of maintaining slaughterhouses is stopped. And although animal killing may sometimes be necessary for survival, at least the mother animal, the cow, should not be killed. That is simply human decency. In the Krsna consciousness movement our practice is that we don't allow the killing of any animals. Krsna says, patram puspam phalam toyam yo me bhaktya prayacchati: "Vegetables, fruits, milk, and grains should be offered to Me in devotion." (Bhagavad-gita 9.26) We take only the remnants of Krsna's food (prasadam). The trees offer us many varieties of fruits, but the trees are not killed. Of course, one living entity is food for another living entity, but that does not mean you can kill your mother for food. Cows are innocent; they give us milk. You take their milk--and then kill them in the slaughterhouse. This is sinful.

Student: Srila Prabhupada, Christianity's sanction of meat-eating is based on the view that lower species of life do not have a soul like the human being's.

Srila Prabhupada: That is foolishness. First of all, we have to understand the evidence of the soul's presence within the body. Then we can see whether the human being has a soul and the cow does not. What are the different characteristics of the cow and the man? If we find a difference in characteristics, then we can say that in the animal there is no soul. But if we see that the animal and the human being have the same characteristics, then how can you say that the animal has no soul? The general symptoms are that the animal eats, you eat; the animal sleeps, you sleep; the animal mates, you mate; the animal defends, and you defend. Where is the difference?

Cardinal Danielou: We admit that in the animal there may be the same type of biological existence as in men, but there is no soul. We believe that the soul is a human soul.

Srila Prabhupada: Our Bhagavad-gita says sarva-yonisu, "In all species of life the soul exists." The body is like a suit of clothes. You have black clothes; I am dressed in saffron clothes. But within the dress you are a human being, and I am also a human being. Similarly, the bodies of the different species are just like different types of dress. There are soul, a part and parcel of God. Suppose a man has two sons, not equally meritorious. One may be a Supreme Court judge and the other may be a common laborer, but the father claims both as his sons. He does not make the distinction that the son who is a judge is very important and the worker-son is not important. And if the judge-son says, "My dear father, your other son is useless; let me cut him up and eat him," will the father allow this?

Cardinal Danielou: Certainly not, but the idea that all life is part of the life of God is difficult for us to admit. There is a great difference between human life and animal life.

Srila Prabhupada: That difference is due to the development of consciousness. In the human body there is developed consciousness. Even a tree has a soul, but a tree's consciousness is not very developed. If you cut a tree it does not resist. Actually, it does resist, but only to a very small degree. There is a scientist named Jagadish Chandra Bose who has made a machine which shows that trees and plants are able to feel pain when they are cut. And we can see directly that when someone comes to kill an animal, it resists, it cries, it makes a horrible sound. So it is a matter of the development of consciousness. But the soul is there within all living beings.

Cardinal Danielou: But metaphysically, the life of man is sacred. Human beings think on a higher platform than the animals do.

Srila Prabhupada: What is that higher platform? The animal eats to maintain his body, and you also eat in order to maintain your body. The cow eats grass in the field, and the human being eats meat from a huge slaughterhouse full of modern machines. But just because you have big machines and a ghastly scene, while the animal simply eats grass, this does not mean that you are so advanced that only within your body is there a soul and that there is not a soul within the body of the animal. That is illogical. We can see that the basic characteristics are the same in the animal and the human being.

Cardinal Danielou: But only in human beings do we find a metaphysical search for the meaning of life.

Srila Prabhupada: Yes. So metaphysically search out why you believe that there is no soul within the animal--that is metaphysics. If you are thinking metaphysically, that's all right. But if you are thinking like an animal, then what is the use of your metaphysical study? Metaphysical means "above the physical" or, in other words, "spiritual." In the Bhagavad-gita Krsna says, sarva-yonisu kaunteya: "In every living being there is a spirit soul." That is metaphysical understanding. Now either you accept Krsna's teachings as metaphysical, or you'll have to take a third-class fool's opinion as metaphysical. Which do you accept?

Cardinal Danielou: But why does God create some animals who eat other animals? There is a fault in the creation, it seems.

Srila Prabhupada: It is not a fault. God is very kind. If you want to eat animals, then He'll give you full facility. God will give you the body of a tiger in your next life so that you can eat flesh very freely. "Why are you maintaining slaughterhouses? I'll give you fangs and claws. Now eat." So the meat-eaters are awaiting such punishment. The animal-eaters become tigers, wolves, cats, and dogs in their next life--to get more facility."

Source
Science of Self-Realization, Chapter 4
Bhaktivedanta Book Trust. HDG A.C. Bhaktivedanta Swami Srila Prabhupada.

27

You Can Eat Meat

But Not From The Slaughterhouse

A Conversation With His Divine Grace A. C. Bhaktivedanta Swami Prabhupada

Jyotirmayi-devi dasi: That priest who visited was telling you that he was asking all his parishioners to follow God's law. So you asked him if he was going to get them to follow the fifth commandment, the law against killing--including animal-killing and especially cow-killing.

Srila Prabhupada: Yes, this is our proposal: "Why should you kill the cow? Let the cow be protected." You can take the cow's milk and use this milk for making so many nutritious, delicious preparations. Aside from that, as far as meat-eating is concerned, every cow will die--so you just wait a while, and there will be so many dead cows. Then you can take all the dead cows and eat. So how is this a bad proposal? If you say, "You are restraining us from

Flash forward to 100 years in the future...

There was a time when life was so barbaric that people ate **animals**!

meat-eating"--no, we don't restrain you. We simply ask you, "Don't kill. When the cow is dead, you can eat it."

Yogesvara dasa: You've pointed out that the cow is just like a mother.

Srila Prabhupada: Yes. She gives us her milk.

Yogesvara dasa: But in the West now, when their parents grow old the people generally send them away to old age homes. So if people have no compassion even toward their own parents, how can we educate them to protect the cow?

Srila Prabhupada: They don't have to protect the cow. We shall protect the cow. Simply we ask them, "Don't purchase meat from the slaughterhouse. We shall supply you the cow after her death." Where is the difficulty?

Satsvarupa dasa Gosvami: Not enough meat fast enough--they're eating so much meat.

Srila Prabhupada: "Not enough"? By killing the cows, how will you get any more meat? The total number of cows will remain the same. Simply wait for their natural death. That is the only restriction. You have got a limited number of cows. Either you wait for their death or you kill them at once--the number of cows is the same. So we simply ask you, "Don't kill them. Wait for their natural death and then take the meat." What is the difficulty? And we simply ask you, "As long as they're alive,

Let's have chicken for dinner.

Thanks for inviting me!

let us take the cow's milk and prepare delicious foods for the whole human society."

Yogesvara dasa: If people don't kill the cows they will have even more meat, because that way the cows will have more time to reproduce more cows. If they don't kill the cows right away, there will be even more cows.

Srila Prabhupada: More cows, yes. They'll have more cows. We simply request, "Don't kill. Don't maintain slaughterhouses." That is very sinful. It brings down very severe karmic reactions upon society. Stop these slaughterhouses. We don't say, "Stop eating meat." You can eat meat, but don't take it from the slaughterhouse, by killing. Simply wait, and you'll get the carcasses.

After all, how long will the cows live? Their maximum age is twenty years, and there are many cows who live only eighteen, sixteen, or ten years. So wait that much time; then regularly get dead cows and eat. What is the difficulty?

~ *Srila Prabhupada (Conversation - Valencey, France, June 1974)*

28

You Can Talk of Peace

Till The Cows Come Home

An Inside Look At The Link Between Cow Slaughter And War.

Winter is again upon us, and again the world staggers through its holy days, raging with quarrel and war. And though we know winter will soon leave us, when, we wonder, will war?

To answer, let's go back some fifty centuries to ancient India, where a white cow and bull are grazing peacefully on the shore of the Sarasvati River. Suddenly, out of the tall grasses, a swarthy, bearded man appears, brandishing a club. He wears the dress of royalty, but when he attacks the innocent cow and bull, he shows himself to be a low-class rogue.

Then the real king appears -- Maharaja Pariksit. With sword upraised, Pariksit addresses the man, with a voice like thunder.

"You rogue, how dare you beat an innocent cow just because Lord Krsna is no longer present? You are a culprit and deserve to be killed!"

Fearing for his life, the man, named Kali, gives up his royal dress and begs the king's mercy. Pariksit spares the mischievous Kali, then banishes him to places of gambling, drinking, prostitution, animal slaughter, and hoarding of gold.

This Kali-Pariksit encounter marked the dawn of what Vedic historians call the Age of Kali, our present age of quarrel and hypocrisy. The Supreme Lord Krsna had just left the earth, and Pariksit was determined to protect the universal religious principles the Lord had revived during His visit. But Kali was just as determined to raise hell; and inexorable time was on his side. As winter follows autumn, so Kali follows Krsna, and the best Pariksit could do was temporarily contain him. Places of gambling, drinking, prostitution, and animal slaughter didn't exist in pious Pariksit's day, but when Kali found gold, he was in business. And so was our age.

Our Age of Kali has come a long way since the first attempt to kill a cow and bull. Gambling, drinking, prostitution, and animal slaughter are big business now, often sanctioned and taxed by the government. Kali's spirit possesses us. Excessive pride has ruined our self-control, and excessive sex our health. Intoxication has destroyed our mercy, lying has obscured the truth, and peace has given way to war.

Kali's spirit of quarrel and hypocrisy pervades even religion, whose mere lip-servers repulse as many as they attract and give God a bad name. Even before church picnics, hayrides, and bingo parties introduce many of us to drinking, sex, and gambling, Kali confirms us as meat-eaters by serving us the flesh of cows. How often have we drunk the cow's milk with one hand and eaten her flesh with the other?

"One who, being fully satisfied by milk, is desirous of killing the cow, is in the grossest ignorance," writes Srila Prabhupada, the founder and spiritual guide of the Hare Krsna movement. "We drink cows' milk; therefore the cow is our mother. And Lord Krsna has created the bull to produce grains for our maintenance; therefore he is our father. Since the bull and cow are our father and mother, how can we kill and eat them? What kind of civilization is this?"

The simple truth of this challenge is lost to most of us. Recently, the American Dairy Association awarded McDonald's, the world's largest restaurant organization, the use of its "REAL" seal, which helps customers distinguish dairy foods from imitations. But Lord Krsna's instructions in the Bhagavad-gita to protect the cow expose the A.D.A. as an imitation dairy association. Why? Because along with an annual 120 million cartons of real milk, 380 million real milk shakes, and 300 million soft-serve ice cream cones and sundaes, McDonald's has handled enough real cow's flesh over the years to sell upwards of 45 billion hamburgers. In other words, instead of protecting the cow, Kali's dairyman is in cahoots with the slaughterhouse.

It is ignorance that compels us to slaughter from 35 to 40 million cows a year. When we buy the nicely-wrapped meat in the market, we have no idea of the suffering we are bringing ourselves by this act. Srila Prabhupada explains:

In this Age of Kali, the propensity for mercy is almost nil. Consequently, there is always fighting and wars between men and nations. Men do not understand that because they unrestrictedly kill so many animals, they also must be slaughtered like animals in big wars. Sometimes during war, soldiers keep their enemies in concentration camps and kill them in very cruel ways. These are reactions brought about by unrestricted animal-killing in the slaughterhouse. As long as human society continues to allow cows to be regularly killed in slaughterhouses, there cannot be any question of peace and prosperity.

Of course, there's always hope for peace, just as, during the bleakest winter, there's still the chance of a sunny day. Kali's clouds of ignorance, thick as they are, cannot yet deny us the truth -- when we see it. And so with this in mind, I would like to tell you about my recent visit to a slaughterhouse.

The pictures on the walls told a story of which Kali must be proud. Around the turn of the century, the founder ran a one-man butchering business. He slaughtered several animals weekly and sold his meat products from a horse-drawn wagon. Then times started to change. Refrigeration, mechanization, the automobile, and two of the founder's sons brought growth to the business. Soon, founder and sons were slaughtering 125 cows weekly, then daily, as they kept gaining more customers and adding more employees and equipment. Over the years, steady growth brought the "packing company" to its present position as the "largest beef slaughterer and fabricator" in the eastern United States.

Kali is so well established that now the king's men federally inspect and grade his slaughtered cows. And for those who can take it, he gives tours.

Rose, my guide, was fortyish, frowsy, and fat as a heifer. Wearing hard hats and smocks we walked out onto a catwalk overlooking the holding pens. A thousand cows bellowed beneath us. The ammonia in the air almost covered the smell of death nearby. Although Rose sounded a little like Dale Evans when she spoke, she sounded even more like the Queen of Hearts.

"We slaughter steers, heifers, and cows -- about 1,300 a day. Would you like to see the stunning?" I nodded, walked through a doorway, and suddenly beheld the most ghastly scene imaginable.

Pistol shots. Cows and bulls upside down. Blood everywhere. What the devil's going on? I looked where Rose was pointing. A man walked over to a Holstein bound to a conveyor, jammed a gun into her forehead, and fired.

"The stunner fires a sliding bolt into the animal's brain," Rose yelled above the din. "Then it's shackled and hoisted -- still alive but insensible to pain. The butcher down there finishes the job by severing the major arteries with a six-inch double-edge sticking knife."

Tongue hanging, eyes bulging, the Holstein rose in the air, kicking and thrashing in her shackle -- obviously fighting for life. Her udder began to spurt milk.

"Just a nervous reaction," Rose assured me. "The body is 'brain dead.'"

The body? What about the struggling soul? What about the progressive journey of all souls back to Godhead? And what about the Supreme Personality of Godhead Himself, Lord Krsna, the soul-giving father of all species?

But Kali runs his religions the same way he runs his wars. Cows and bulls, like enemies, have no souls. They're subhuman, nonpersons. Kill them.

The stunner, his eyes black pools under a white hard hat, reloaded his pistol. He and the butcher were killing better than a hundred cows an hour and, according to Vedic literature, preparing a dark future for themselves: "Cow killers are condemned to rot in hellish life for as many thousands of years as there are hairs on the body of the cow." But there was no need to tell anyone here they were going to hell. Awash with blood, the "Kill Floor" made the Bible's lake of fire look like Palm Springs.

It was hard for me to keep talking to Rose as though everything was all right. Kali's men held big knives, and Maharaja Pariksit was nowhere in sight. As we walked through blood puddles, my only sword was a pen.

"After the kill, the animals are dehided by a stripper, eviscerated, split into sides, weighed, and shrouded for chilling in the coolers."

Nazi and Soviet death camps never enjoyed such efficiency or such good public relations. And why not? The public's dinner table is the last stop on the production line.

"You have just dined," wrote Emerson, "and however scrupulously the slaughterhouse is concealed in the graceful distance of miles, there is complicity."

We passed into the "Fabrication Plant," where workers boned and trimmed the meat for packaging. Their faces showed many different extractions, a kind of General Assembly of butchers. I thought of the United Nations, of how its buildings stand on the very spot where New York City slaughterhouses used to, and of how its members have failed to keep the peace.

A prime example is the Middle East, where destiny has embroiled Christians, Moslems, and Jews -- the world's "religious" meat-eaters -- in a perennial paradigm of hatred and war. The peoples to whom the Lord delivered the Old Testament, New Testament, and Koran are always reinterpreting His words to suit their appetites. Now, "Thou shall not kill," conveniently reads, "Thou shall not commit murder," and the Moslem's and the Jew's "ritual slaughter" of fully conscious cows turns out to be more cruel than the "humane" stun-killing of the Christian. But the Lord is pleased with neither. And war in the Middle East -- and everywhere else -- continues.

Watching mother cow and father bull become man's meat -- horrible as it was -- left no doubt about the connection between slaughter and war. The misapplied technology that increased the slaughter in the founder's "packing company" also increased the slaughter in World Wars 1 and II. And the dues owed since then are in the billions.

Back home from the slaughterhouse, I walked among our Hare Krsna farm's Brown Swiss cows and bulls, who welcomed me with licks and nudges. We looked up as a military jet thundered across the sky. Even if an atomic war doesn't come, I reflected, only Krsna consciousness can release us from the slaughterhouse of repeated birth and death. And if enough of us become Krsna conscious, then even communists and capitalists can learn how to protect cows and live peacefully during Kali's wintry age of discontent.

By Suresvara dasa

29

Karma of the Nation

In studying the science of karma as outlined in the Vedic texts, we must remember that it is actually a basic law of physics, or as Newton's third law of motion states, that for every action there is an equal and opposite reaction. On the universal scale it is also a natural law, only it is called the law of karma. Individuals acquire karma as a result of their good or bad activities. Pious actions will result in positive or uplifting reactions in the future. Impious or nefarious actions will bring about negative, unwanted or troublesome reactions to endure in the future. This is to provide the necessary lessons to learn what we should or should not do, which can then balance our karma and our consciousness. However, not only do individuals have or acquire specific karma, but also a collective karma can be acquired by whole societies, or nations, depending on the overall activities of the citizens.

In understanding national karma, we can consider how the Manu-samhita (8.304-309) describes how a king or ruler of a country receives one sixth of the total karma of the subjects he rules. This, of course, depends on the general activities of the citizens. If the majority of people are pious and spiritually oriented, and the ruler protects those citizens to maintain a peaceful society in which such people can flourish, then the king will also share in the good activities and good karma of the citizens. Otherwise, if the ruler does not properly protect and maintain the citizens but allows criminals to run loose and create havoc, while still collecting taxes from the people, the overall karma will be extremely dark. Such a ruler will take upon himself the foulness of his countrymen and sink into hell.

From this description, we can see that if the ruler is so much affected by the total karma of the citizens of the country, then the nation itself fosters its future according to the good or bad activities of the citizens. So whatever reactions this country will endure in its future, whether it be harvests of plenty, good economy, or starvation from famine and drought, or victory over our enemies or destruction from war, depends on the way we live today.

History has noted many countries and civilizations in the past who, although seeming to be so powerful while living a frivolous, decadent, and spoiled lifestyle, finally met their doom. Such a downfall was usually quite unexpected at the time. However, by understanding the law of karma, such a collapse can be fairly predictable. We can see this in the analysis of the Roman Empire.

The last great civilization in the West was the Roman Empire, of which historians have noted five characteristics that helped cause that great society to fall apart. First, there was a love of show and luxury. Everyone was eager to acquire material things as a sign of affluence. This also helped cause the second factor, which was a widening gap between the very rich and the very poor.

The third factor was a complete obsession with sex. In the latter days of the Roman Empire, sex became the sole interest, whether in ordinary conversations, or in art, culture--everything. Pompeii was a big resort for this kind of licentious living and sex. (And we all know of the earthquake in A.D. 69 that damaged Pompeii, and then the volcanic eruption in A.D. 79 that finally buried it.)

A fourth factor in the downfall of the Roman Empire was a freakishness and abandonment in the arts which masqueraded and pretended to be originality. This can easily be found now in modern art, music, sculpture, etc.

The fifth factor was the creation of the welfare state and the increasing desire amongst the people to live off the government. Even today, there are places where anyone can get welfare and not have to work. Plus, with more sex, the more children that are born, which entitles the welfare recipient to more money.

We should carefully regard these points and take note of where our modern nations stand because history repeats itself. We presently find an increase in these same things everywhere. For example, almost all advertising nowadays evolves around the idea of having or getting sex appeal, no matter whether it is in buying a car, or buying anything that people are told they need, or attaining a successful career. And it does not take much to figure out why everyone wants sex appeal. So the present times merely reflect attitudes and changes that have taken place before, as in the Roman Empire.

For example, modern philosophy, whether in sociology, psychology, art, politics, the sciences, etc., usually presents the idea that there is no absolute law or standard. In other words, whatever turns you on, do it; whatever you believe in, it's O.K. There is no absolute, and anyone who thinks there is becomes regarded as a fanatic. Similarly, in the Roman Empire, there was no emphasis on God or faith in moral standards. There were many denominations, but the attitude was anyone could believe anything he wanted. But those who were serious about their religion were severely persecuted.

In the case of the Christians, they were thrown to the lions in the amphitheaters as a spectator sport. The people would watch in the stands and applaud the utter brutality of it all. One reason for this was that the Christians refused to accept the Roman gods. They believed in only one God as a pure, infinite being who set down the law, which if not followed would cause one to go to hell. Romans accepted gods who drank wine, ate meat, had sex, and so on. Therefore, Romans looked on Christians as if they were fanatics. This is the same way modern philosophers, politicians, and liberals today look at people who seem to be overly dedicated to a law of God, such as the law of karma. Rather than understanding the law of karma, such people would rather criticize it and simply carry on with their frivolous and whimsical habits, while remaining ignorant of the consequences.

We should point out, however, that karma is not a belief system but is a science. One may believe that he can do whatever he wants and that there is no jail house, but if he acts like a criminal and gets caught and thrown into confinement, then he will be forced to adjust his thinking and face the results of his activities. Similarly, people may think they can escape the universal laws and do whatever they like, but when they are forced by the law of karma to face their destined punishments either in this life, or after death or in a future life, it will be too late.

When we see, therefore, that people in certain areas of the country are suffering from drought, that farmers cannot grow their crops, that fires are consuming vast forests and destroying homes, that storms are causing destruction and devastation to cities and towns, or incurable diseases are affecting more and more people all the time, or when other countries threaten us with war, we should not miss the message. It is easy to ask ourselves, "Why has God done this to me?" or "Why has He allowed this to happen?" and then try to put the blame on someone else. But why should such reversals in life not happen to us? What have we done to avoid it? Usually nothing. Therefore, we must understand how the law of karma affects everyone.

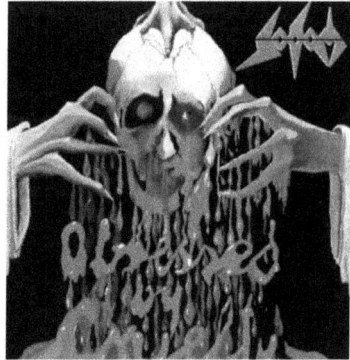

When we stop to consider that as many as 134 million animals and 3 billion birds are slaughtered every year in one country alone, and hundreds of thousands more are tortured and killed for useless scientific experiments, is it any wonder why there should not be a heavy reaction to the cries of pain from so many innocent living beings as they are butchered in order to satisfy mankind's thoughtless cravings? Everyone wants to be happy and live in peace, but how can this be peace when so many other entities suffer from the most painful experiments in so-called scientific laboratories? Or are methodically killed each day at slaughterhouses so that their corpses can be sold in supermarkets? But it is not just commercial enterprises that do this, but it is also the government. In 1986, the Office of Technology Assessment

CLOSE *all*

SLAUGHTERHOUSES

"The first time I went there and returned home, I cried for two days; I hid all the knives, I wanted to die"

Georges Franju, film-maker and director of the documentary "The Blood of the Beast" shot at a slaughterhouse in Paris in 1949.

reported that 84% of all painful animal experimentation is carried out by the military. The "In Defense of Animals" group also stated that of 22 military bases, 83,389 animals were used in 1987, and 142,735 in 1988, of which pain was used in 99% of the experiments on dogs, 81% on cats, and 43% on primates. And there is no public outcry about this?

This does not include the widespread torture of people by people. Political prisoners are often tortured by rulers or their military to keep people in line with the particular agenda of the regime. Some leaders have such a mentality that they enjoy keeping their subjects in a miserable condition. Or there is torture and fighting of people for being of a different religion. This type of thing goes on much more than we think, and has been going on for hundreds of years.

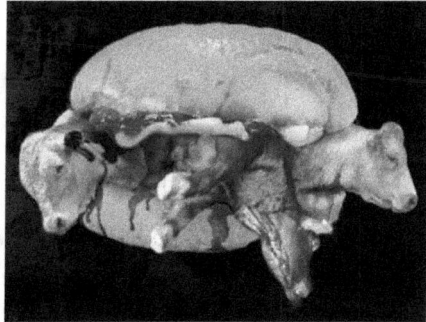

Therefore, when society in general has such a cruel and callous attitude towards other living entities, or are too wasteful in regards to the planet's natural resources, or live an unnecessarily decadent or frivolous lifestyle, nature arranges reactions in various ways to humble us, or teach us a lesson. One of which is in the form of wars. From time to time we all have to watch as we ship our young men and women off to be killed or maimed in the slaughterhouse of war. As long as there are large numbers of innocent animals being unnecessarily killed and tortured day after day throughout the year, there will never be peace for long, for war will always exist somewhere, in which we will be forced to become involved.

But war also means war in the family, such as discontent, arguments, separation, and divorce; war in the community, such as gang wars, crime, robberies, murders, and rape; and industrial and economic wars as well as international wars and terrorism. These reactions affect many millions of people every day around the world, and it is nothing more than the workings of nature as it reflects the consciousness of the people who inhabit this world.

We must stop eating animals to even begin realizing our spiritual identity and purpose. Comments? Call Tom (313) 434-5121

When the majority of people in a country are influenced by commercialism and addicted to the four most karmically implicating activities--meat-eating, intoxication, illicit sex, and gambling--there will definitely be reactions to endure in the future. This is the universal law. There is no amount of economic planning, defense buildup, agricultural arrangement, or even weather forecasting that will help us to avoid unexpected karmic reactions. If the ruler of a country receives one-sixth of the aggregate good or bad karma of the citizens, then the citizens themselves will also experience the reactions that the country is destined to receive, as arranged by nature.

By understanding the law of karma and abiding by the four principles which are especially recommended for this age--namely, truthfulness, cleanliness, austerity, and mercy--the people (and the leaders) will surely become strong, develop good moral character, be concerned for the welfare of all others, acquire a sound state of mind, and will attain a great destiny like no other country in the world. We all want to make this world

a better place, and there is a method which will enable us to do that, which we are revealing. But we must understand that there is more to it than the obvious plan-making that goes on amongst our politicians, economic advisors, judiciaries, etc. There is the subtle aspect that goes on and is determined by the decisions and activities of each and every individual. Therefore, those who take the time to understand the law of karma and try to abide by it can certainly be understood to be people who are working for a better future, not only for themselves, but for a better world.

(By Stephen Knapp)

The Author

Dr. Sahadeva dasa (Sanjay Shah) is a monk in vaisnava tradition. His areas of work include research in Vedic and contemporary thought, Corporate and educational training, social work and counselling, travelling, writing books and of course, practicing spiritual life and spreading awareness about the same.

He is also an accomplished musician, composer, singer, instruments player and sound engineer. He has more than a dozen albums to his credit so far. (SoulMelodies.com)

His varied interests include alternative holistic living, Vedic studies, social criticism, environment, linguistics, history, art & crafts, nature studies, web technologies etc.

Many of his books have been acclaimed internationally and translated in other languages.

By The Same Author

Oil-Final Countdown To A Global Crisis And Its Solutions

End of Modern Civilization And Alternative Future

To Kill Cow Means To End Human Civilization

Cow And Humanity - Made For Each Other

Cows Are Cool - Love 'Em!

Let's Be Friends - A Curious, Calm Cow

Wondrous Glories of Vraja

We Feel Just Like You Do

Tsunami Of Diseases Headed Our Way - Know Your Food Before Time Runs Out

Cow Killing And Beef Export - The Master Plan To Turn India Into A Desert

Capitalism Communism And Cowism - A New Economics For The 21st ` Century

Noble Cow - Munching Grass, Looking Curious And Just Hanging Around

World - Through The Eyes Of Scriptures

To Save Time Is To Lengthen Life

Life Is Nothing But Time - Time Is Life, Life Is Time

Lost Time Is Never Found Again

Spare Us Some Carcasses - An Appeal From The Vultures

An Inch of Time Can Not Be Bought With A Mile of Gold

Cow Dung For Food Security And Survival of Human Race

Cow Dung - A Down To Earth Solution To Global Warming And Climate Change

Career Women - The Violence of Modern Jobs And The Lost Art of Home Making

Working Moms And Rise of A Lost Generation

Glories of Thy Wondrous Name

India A World Leader in Cow Killing And Beef Export - An Italian Did It In 10 Years

If Violence Must Stop, Slaughterhouses Must Close Down

Peak Soil - Industrial Civilization, On The Verge of Eating Itself

Corporatocracy : The New Gods - Greedy, Ruthless And Reckless

(More information on availability on DrDasa.com)

www.ingramcontent.com/pod-product-compliance
Lightning Source LLC
Chambersburg PA
CBHW060500280326
41933CB00014B/2801